RD

# FRAU

dangerous theories



## 1000 YEARS WITH INFLATION AS A POLICY

Rune Østgård
Fyrgata 3
7714 Steinkjer
Norway
rune@advokatostgard.no
(+47) 905 09 419
www.undoqo.com


ISBN: 979-83-671069-9-2

Editor: Rune Østgård
Cover graphics: Mattis Storhaug
English translation: Ingrid Elise Østgård and Scott Baker-Marflitt

Font: Calibri 10/12

*In memory of Eindride*

*We shall not grow wiser*

*before we learn*

*that much that we have done*

*was very foolish*

*

Friedrich August von Hayek

**Praise for *Fraudcoin: 1000 Years with Inflation*:**

*This is an incredibly important book. It lays out the story of inflation as a policy in a clear, precise, and easy-to-understand way. It's the story of how you and everyone you know have been duped. Deceived. That we have been deceived for centuries, continue to be today. That money as we know it – the very foundation of how we organize, motivate and reward, what we measure everything against, what we use to store value – does not serve the interests of the people, but on the contrary is a very effective tool for confiscating wealth. It is absolutely necessary for a healthy society to have healthy money, but that will not happen until most people understand what sound money is, and why the inflation policy creates sick money.*
**@hodlonaut**

*I am greatly impressed by this book, which provides insight into what is fundamental to understanding how destructive inflation is. It should definitely become a bestseller*
**Johan Petter Nystuen, Professor Emeritus of Geology, Ås, Norway**

*An extremely well written book that explains everything you need to know about inflation, in addition to presenting solutions*
**Lars M. Haugen, investor, Oslo, Norway**

*The book is a future classic. It brings out the points in a clear and understandable way. It is comparable to one of my favorites, the award-winning 'Economix'*
**Ronny Christie Kleverud, pedagogical assistant, Drammen, Norway**

*It's the best book that I have ever read. It gives an excellent overview of the history of money, and has an interesting critique of our monetary system*
**Lars Berg-Hansen, entrepreneur, *Bindal, Norway***

*It was a delight to read this book and I hope it will create a much-needed debate on our monetary policy*
**Robert Pedersen, senior physician, Levanger, Norway**

*This is the most important book in many years in Norway*
**Gregard Mikkelborg, owner of *Gull er Penger*, Oslo, Norway**

*A high quality, easy to read book about rampaging inflation, with a good portion of history*
**Andreas Kjærstad, farmer, Bindal, Norway**

*This book is dedicated to my beloved family, my mother Eva, who gave me the best one can get, a loving and safe upbringing, my oldest sister Ingrid Elise, for her good mood, drive and care for everyone around her, my youngest sister Gunvor Helene, for her infectious laughter, empathy and dedication to quality in everything that she does, my mother-in-law Oddbjørg, who is worth her weight in gold, my partner Astrid, who gives me security, stability, joy and who dares to be the critic on whom I depend so that I do not derail and disappear too much into the world of wonder, our daughter Milda, for being the light of our life, and for being a daily reminder of what can be achieved with courage, faith and willpower, and Ingrid Elise's partner, Scott, for treating me as a brother.*

*Rune*

# Preface

A little more than 100 years ago, the famous British economist John Maynard Keynes wrote this about inflation:

> By this means the government may secretly and unobserved, confiscate the wealth of the people, and not one man in a million will detect the theft.

One could thus be of the impression that the topic is complex and that it is not possible to understand what is happening. Fortunately, that is not correct.

Inflation is a policy, and as we shall see, it is very easy to understand both the policy and its consequences.

Steinkjer, October 2022

Rune Østgård

# Introduction

**The purpose of this book**

Many people are worried about inflation, wondering what causes it and what effect it can have on society. Inflation is very simple, and this book aims to explain it as such. It focuses on **the big picture**, and we only go into the details to the extent necessary to understand what inflation actually is.

The book addresses two main themes. The first being how the present monetary policy affects society, and the second maps out the theory that some economists developed in the beginning of the 20th century that a little inflation is good for the economy. My goal is that by reading this book you will understand inflation policy so precisely that you are able to reflect independently on this. In the introduction, we look at some key concepts, including what money and inflation are, and summarize the topics addressed in the book.

**What is the origin of the word inflation?**

The word "inflation" derives from the Latin "inflare", in English "inflate", which means to pump up, increase, expand. It refers to "money inflation", which means an increase or expansion of the money supply, while "price inflation" is the same as a general rise in prices. Normally, you must increase the money supply in order to get a general price increase.

**What is money?**

Money can be described as something that is a *universal medium of exchange,* that is, something that can be used to trade all manner of goods and services. It is commonly understood that money, among other things, must have the following characteristics:

(1) They must constitute a *measure or metric,* such as ten dollar, five Norwegian kroner, or one ounce (31.1 grams)
(2) They need to be *able to store a value* so you can use them for both trading and saving

The dominant view throughout history has been that the value of money must remain *stable.* If the money loses purchasing power as time passes, the money cannot be saved for later use and thus the requirement in paragraph (2) above will not be met.

Jon Nicolaisen, Deputy Governor of Norges Bank, the Norwegian central bank, gave a speech to the *Norwegian Academy of Science* in 2017 in which he said that money must have a "fairly" stable value. Sveriges Riksbank, the Swedish central bank, states on its website that "We ensure that money retains its value over time." Andreas Granath wrote in his article *Central Banks Claim to Preserve the Value of Money through Inflation*, published on mises.org on September 29th, 2022:

> [I] sent an email to the Riksbank about this and asked them how they could possibly make such a statement, and how they define the term "value". A week later I received an answer where they said that by "money retaining its value" they mean that the Consumer Price Index (CPI) should steadily increase in a "slow" pace (2 percent per year). "Most other central banks, like the FED define price stability in this way", they added.

The fact that this is most governments' and central banks' policy is the dominant theme of the book. The question is – why don't states want the value to be kept *stable*, period?

**The historical difference between money and currency**

Before people started using money, we bartered or bargained for trade. Some goods proved to be more suitable as a medium of exchange than others, and these, therefore, gradually developed a monetary function. Over time, pieces of rare metals were the goods that became most popular to use in exchange for other things. The Kingdom of Lydia, located in present-day Turkey, began producing coins that they called *stater* approximately 600 BCE. These consisted of electrum, which is a natural alloy of gold and silver. Later, copper, silver and gold coins became common means of payment throughout most of the world.

There is an important distinction between physical assets such as gold coins on the one hand, and paper values and the electronic money in your online banking account on the other. Copper, silver, and gold have historically been regarded as money, while banknotes, for example, have been regarded as a representation of money, which can be more widely defined as "currency". Banknotes were a representation of money, because the bearer could originally go to the bank and demand to have them exchanged for a predetermined quantity of valuable metals, typically in the form of a certain number of coins. The 50-dollar bill and the numbers that show what you have deposited in your online bank, are therefore, in financial terms, currency. The earliest well-documented use of banknotes as a means of payment dates from around the year 800 BCE during the Tang Dynasty in China.

The difference between money and currency is primarily that money preserves its value, that is to say, its purchasing power, while currency does not.

The reason why money preserves its value is as a result of the natural scarcity of valuable metals. Additionally, it requires a great deal of prospecting, engineering and processing in order to extract the metals. The growth in the supply of gold is particularly low. The annual average increase in the amount of gold, globally, is about 1.5 percent, which is about the same as the population growth. Comparatively, almost nothing is required to create currency, for example by printing banknotes. The growth of currency varies from country to country and over time. For instance, average annual increase in the money in circulation in the US was eight percent during the period 1959-1973, which can be compared with a 38 percent increase we saw over a two-year period during the COVID-19 pandemic.

The price of oil illustrates how well money keeps its purchasing power compared with currency. A barrel of oil cost 1.44 grams of gold in 1946, while it cost only 1.28 grams of gold in 2021. By comparison, one barrel of oil cost 8 kroner in 1946, and 662 kroner in 2021. This means that oil has become 12.5% cheaper when measured in gold and 83 times more expensive with respect to kroner.

**The big picture** here is that money (gold) keeps its purchasing power, while the currency's purchasing power drops dramatically. This is not new knowledge. The French philosopher Voltaire said in 1729 that "all paper money returns to its intrinsic value, that is, zero."

It is a long time since people understood the difference between money and currency, and today it is not common for most people to distinguish, by definition, between the two. Therefore, to make it easier for the reader, in this book we use *money* as a common term, which includes what used to be money historically, and *currency*, which is what we use as a means of payment today.

**Why do we have price inflation?**

In a free market, forces of demand and supply determine the prices of commodities and the changes therein. If the demand of a commodity increases and the supply remains the same, the price will increase. However, a general price increase is normally not something that happens in a free market.

The reason why *general price inflation* is common is that the government *wants* price increases. In other words, they want money to lose some value, and therefore, *inflation is a policy*. This is also the reason why Nicolaisen said in his speech that the value of money must be kept "fairly" stable. States achieve price inflation by ensuring that more money enters into circulation.

In his book *What You should know about Inflation*, the American economist Henry Hazlitt explained what happens:

> When the supply of money is increased, people have more money to offer for goods. If the supply of goods does not increase — or does not increase as much as the supply of money — then the prices of goods will go up. Each individual dollar becomes less valuable because there are more dollars. Therefore, more of them will be offered against, say, a pair of shoes or a hundred bushels of wheat than before. A "price" is an exchange ratio between a dollar and a unit of goods. When people have more dollars, they value each dollar less. Goods then rise in price, not because goods are scarcer than before, but because dollars are more abundant.

Prices will increase the most in areas where the influx of new money is large. Therefore, in a country with a large increase in the money supply, prices rise more than in a country with a small increase in the money supply. Nicolaus Copernicus, best known for being an astronomer, wrote about this as early as in the 16th century. The same applies within individual countries. In regions where the influx of new money is large, prices will rise more than in regions where the influx of new money is small.

**How is new money created today?**

When we consider how important money is to us as individuals and society, it is a great paradox that so few people know what money and inflation is. Even fewer people know how money is created. Nor do many economists know how new money is created or indeed how great the growth of the money supply actually is, i.e., how much new money is created over time.

Today, money is essentially created in four different ways. They are the same types of money, in the sense that they are all, for example, US dollars or Norwegian kroner and that they can be used on an equal footing as a universal medium of exchange, but the way they are created allows us to give them the following collective terms:

- Cash
- Bank money
- Emergency money for banks
- Emergency money for others, otherwise known as "helicopter money"

In addition to these four types of money, the central bank regularly provides financial markets with money by lending to commercial banks. This is something that central banks have traditionally done, among other things, to regulate how big reserves the banks have with the central bank.

These four types of money have in common that they are *de facto* "created out of nothing". This means that governments increase the money supply without being tied to or based on real or quantifiable values such as gold or silver. Nor is the holder of, for example, a 50-dollar bill entitled to exchange the note for any reserves that the banks may have.

*Bank money* is created by ordinary banks when they give loans to customers. It thus means that they are created when someone incurs debts. This type of money can therefore also be said to be created by *credit*.

It is bank money that we have the most of. This means that most of our money has been created through debts incurred by governments, private companies, and citizens. The more loans we take out, the more money we create. The more debt we have in our society, the more money we have in circulation.

The counterpart to the increase in the money supply when banks lend is that it is also reduced when borrowers repay their loans. In a year, banks usually lend more than borrowers repay. Therefore, the money supply increases almost continuously, in step with growing debt.

The other two "types" of money, i.e., emergency money for banks and emergency money for others, are created by central banks. We'll go through this in depth later in the chapter *The Money's Journey*.

Throughout the book, I occasionally turn to the statistics for the growth of what is called “the broad money supply M2”. It includes funds that private individuals, non-profit organizations, municipalities, and businesses that are not banks, as well as other financial institutions can easily use for payment, such as cash, bank deposits and what are called certificates of deposit and money market funds.

**Fiat money system**

The monetary system that we have today is called a “fiat” monetary system. Deriving from Latin, “fiat”, it means “let it happen”. The reason for giving the monetary system this name is that you create money out of nothing and at the same time decide that it should be accepted as the universal means of payment. Only the state can establish this type of money. That is, fiat money, unlike, for example, silver or gold, is not something that develops into a means of payment through voluntary transactions in a free society.

Introducing fiat money is a special form of exercise of governmental power. This is akin to how kings previously established property rights over what had previously been ownerless lands or lands belonging to Indigenous peoples. They then made it known through *royal decree* that the land now belonged to the king. Property rights then arose as if by miracle, created out of nothingness. By comparison, private individuals must *use* ownerless land for them to become owners.

If private individuals are to create money, it must be done by voluntarily starting to use something as a means of payment. For example, people used livestock, such as goats and camels, as a means of payment many thousands of years BCE. Money then developed naturally because of voluntary actions, and not because of someone deciding that something should be money.

**Trust and money**

When economists discuss fiat money, we often hear them say that the system is based on trust or that it is "solely based on trust". For instance, the Bank of England has published an article on its website, updated May 19th, 2020, *Why does money depend on trust?,* that states that "The reason money works when you pay for things is because people trust in its value."

However, the question we need to ask ourselves is the following: If the government *coerces* its citizens to use its currency, or citizens don't understand anything about how the monetary system works, nor how it effects the economy, is it correct to say that the system is based on *trust*?

**Legal and compulsory tender**

Legal and compulsory tender rules vary from country to country. Each country has commonality insofar as these states require that taxes must be paid with the country's currency. This coercive provision gives the country's currency a privileged status which normally means that the country's currency will also be used as the country's universal medium of exchange. The laws do not usually prohibit citizens and businesses from agreeing to use other types of means of payment.

**The deposit guarantees**

Governments require banks to contribute to a fund that guarantees or underwrites bank deposits. One of the aims is to give people confidence in banks and the banking system.

If the bank slips into bankruptcy, this arrangement in the US covers up to 250,000 USD per depositor, per bank. In Norway, it covers up to 2 million NOK and in the EU up to 100,000 EUR.

The problem with these schemes is that the guarantee funds only have sufficient funds to cover a small proportion of what customers together have in accounts in banks. The reason for this is that the schemes are significantly underfunded. And the reason they are underfunded is that the banks have wanted it to be this way, and politicians have accepted it. In Norway, for example, the requirement is that the fund must only have liquid assets that is proportional to at least 0.8% of total guaranteed deposits. If a collapse in the banking industry wipes out as little as 1%

of deposits in Norway, the fund will therefore only have enough liquid funds to replace 80% of what customers are entitled to.

Deposit guarantees do not provide security against a reduction of the value of the money due to price inflation, even if the money becomes worthless. When the banking sector is in danger and people queue up to withdraw their money, it is quite common for the authorities to let banks close or refuse to allow people access to their deposits, as is the case in Lebanon at the time of writing. In practice, the accounts are frozen, while inflation eats up the value of the deposits, whilst at the same time the bank is protected from bankruptcy.

**Reserve requirements**

Previously, governments decided that banks had to set aside a proportionate amount as a reserve in the central bank for each loan they agreed with their customers. This is something that many states, including, for example, the United States, the United Kingdom, and Norway, have recently abandoned. Instead, the rules include provisions that set requirements for banks' equity capital and other factors that provide an indication of how healthy banks' finances should be.

**The quantity paradox**

With fiat money, the total value of money in circulation in society does not rise by increasing the money supply. For example, if we double the number of dollars in circulation by showering the country with dollars from a helicopter, then those who sell goods and services merely double the prices. In other words, fiat money doesn't increase its worth more when society gets more of it. Instead, everyone's money loses its value in the marketplace.

It logically follows that every time an ordinary bank or central bank creates more dollars, they "dilute" the value of all the other dollars that already exists. This means, among other things, that if central banks say that there is a crisis, and that they must print new money to give emergency money to the banks to "save the economy", then it is not the central bank, but all of us who take the cost. It is also we who save the banks from bankruptcy. Whether we "save the economy" in this way is a topic that we will also touch on.

Since new fiat money reduces the value of the other money in circulation, it is natural in economic terms to compare it with other things that have negative value, such as pollution. In economic theory of pollution, it is general agreement that it is the polluter who must pay. This does not apply to monetary policy. Here, the opposite principle applies, i.e., everyone must bear the costs when someone "pollutes".

When it is valuable metals that are the money in a society, the growth of the money supply will also produce growth in wealth. The more gold Norway has, the more we can purchase in terms of real economic goods domestically as well as from imports. However, it also applies to such money, that it will have a diminishing value if it accumulates within a geographically delineated area, and it is difficult to spend the money outside of this area. The value of the gold coins falls, as you must pay more for the goods and services when you buy something.

**The pyramid scheme**

The combining factors that it is primarily bank lending that determines the money supply, and that borrowers must repay the loans with interest, means that the money supply must grow continuously. If the money supply does not grow, there will not be enough money to pay the interest. A fiat money system therefore presupposes a constant increase in the money supply.

The system bears a certain resemblance to pyramid schemes. In a pyramid scheme, there is a participant who starts the game, who "sits on top" and who enlists other people who "sit below". Those who sit below give money to the person at the top, but in return they can enlist others who end up further down the pyramid. Once they've got enough people under them, it's their turn to receive money from those below. The pyramid expands further longitudinally and latitudinally so that it gradually becomes taller and wider. It stops when those at the bottom are unable to enlist more people to participate. Those who end up at the bottom therefore find that they have only paid someone further up the pyramid, without themselves receiving any recompense, because they have not managed to enlist enough people under them. The lower they are on the pyramid, the more they lose. Needless to say, pyramid schemes are illegal.

The fiat money system can then also be described as a pyramid. The central bank sits at the top, and it decides how much money will be released into society. Just below the top are the banks, which the central bank allows to create new money through lending. Below that we find the loan customers, who receive the new money. For customers to both repay their loans and get interest paid to banks, banks need to get customers to take out ever more loans, so that the money supply (pyramid) continues to grow. If growth in the money supply comes to a halt, the system would collapse because there is a lack of money to pay interest.

The consequence of this is also that, if interest rates go up, an even greater increase in the money supply is required to pay both interest and instalments. The problem is that higher interest rates will lead to fewer people taking out loans, therefore the money supply will not increase as much. The system works in such a way that one is constantly dependent on interest rates being kept artificially low, and on increasing the money supply little by little, over time, instead of increasing it substantially and suddenly.

If one compares this with a society that uses gold as money, the money supply will grow very little. The market mechanism, where the supply and demand for money loans determine how high interest rates will be, ensures that the loan market does not lay claim to a larger share of society's total money supply. Other than that, there is always enough money available in society for borrowers to pay both interest and instalments without being dependent on others having to take out new loans.

**How the value of money develops over time**

How has the value of, for example, the US dollar and the Norwegian krone performed historically? One way of assessing this is to look at the countries' official statistics on changes in the cost of living, i.e., the consumer price index.

The short story is that prices are 30 times higher in dollar value now in 2022 compared to 1913, the year before World War I broke out. Measured in Norwegian kroner, prices are 65 times higher now than in 1913. Before and during this period, the monetary system has varied considerably, which has also affected the value of money. Since 1878, both countries have had the so-called *gold standard* and the *gold exchange standard*, while since 1973 they have had a system based on *pure fiat money.*

The table below shows how the value of dollars and kroner has evolved when measured against official figures on the cost of living under different monetary systems.

*Table: Value of US dollar / Norwegian krone as measured against CPI 1879 – 2022*

| ***Year*** | ***Monetary system USA*** | ***US dollar*** | ***Monetary system Norway*** | ***Norwegian krone*** |
|---|---|---|---|---|
| 1879 | Gold standard | 1,01 | Gold standard | 0,74 |
| **1913** | **Gold standard (before WWI)** | **1** | **Gold standard (before WWI)** | **1** |
| 1928 | Gold standard | 1,73 | Gold exchange standard 1 | 1,68 |
| 1930 | Gold standard | 1,69 | Gold exchange standard 1 | 1,65 |
| 1934 | Gold Standard (devalued) | 1,35 | Fiat, pegged to pound | 1,47 |
| 1945 | Gold exchange standard 2 | 4 | Gold exchange standard 2 | 8 |
| 1965 | Gold exchange standard 2 | 4 | Gold exchange standard 2 | 8 |
| 1972 | Gold exchange standard 2 | 4 | Gold exchange standard 2 | 8 |

| | | | | |
|---|---|---|---|---|
| 1973 | Fiat | 4,48 | Fiat | 8,53 |
| 1974 | Fiat | 4,98 | Fiat | 9,42 |
| **2022** | **Fiat** | **30** | **Fiat** | **65** |

**The big picture** is as follows:

- With the gold standard, the value of the dollar was stable, while the krone depreciated slightly
- With the gold exchange standard, both the dollar and the krone depreciated more than with the gold standard
- Both the dollar and the krone lost a great deal of their value after the governments switched to a pure fiat money system
- The krone lost more and more in value compared to the dollar in the period after 1913
- The loss in value was twice as big for the krone as for the dollar after the countries introduced a pure fiat standard from 1973

This means that the type of monetary system affects the value of money a great deal. We will return to the development of monetary systems in the next chapter.

**Hyperinflation**

Hyperinflation refers to a situation where price inflation has spiraled out of control. It is a prerequisite for hyperinflation that the state forces the nation to use fiat money and that the state ensures a significant expansion of the money supply. The example that is perhaps best known is from Germany in the early 1920s, during the so-called *Weimar Republic*. Then the banknotes became so little worth that you may as well have set fire to it. The people were forced to return to a barter economy, the decay of societal norms and the hastening of poverty everywhere.

There has been hyperinflation in many countries throughout history. Today, residents of Lebanon and Zimbabwe are affected by this. Here are the official figures (in percentage) for inflation in selected countries as of June 2022:

Lebanon – 210

Zimbabwe – 196

Turkey – 73.5

Sri Lanka – 54.6

Estonia – 21.9

Russia – 15.9

Spain – 10.8

EU – 9.6

USA – 9.1

Germany – 7.5

Norway – 6.3

France – 6.1

Switzerland – 3.4

As we can see, there is a broad range, between so-called "modern states" in the equally confected concept of “The West”, even though all of them have a fiat money system. This shows that *the way* in which monetary policy is conducted based on fiat money also has a lot to say.

With these levels of price inflation, the value of money in Lebanon and Zimbabwe will be halved in about 3 months, while the half-life in the EU and the US will be about 7 years. Over the past year, inflation has risen over most of the world, and is far higher than it used to be. In the US and Norway, for example, it is 4.5 and 3 times higher, respectively, than the official target of 2%. We have never had global hyperinflation, but there is a real possibility that it could happen in the not-too-distant future.

**What is the history of inflation as a policy?**

The Athenian city-state adopted a combination of taxation and inflation as a policy almost 2,500 years ago to finance the war against Sparta. The Roman Emperors used the same template almost 2,000 years ago to finance the expansion of the Roman Empire. The Norwegian Viking, King Harald Hardråde, did the same when he tried to conquer England almost 1,000 years ago. Inflation as a policy contributed to the fall of Athens, the Roman Empire, and prompted the end of the Viking Age. The historical development serves as a useful guide, and I will place a lot of emphasis upon it, focusing on what has happened over the past 1,000 years.

**The economists**

Previously, economists agreed that inflation was bad for society. Those who claimed otherwise were viewed with great suspicion. From the beginning of the 20th century, several economists began to argue that inflation was good. During the 1920’s and 1930’s, politicians preferred to listen to economists who supported inflation. These economists also ended up gaining the most important positions in the governmental bodies and universities. Several economists who continued to argue that inflation was dangerous were given the cold shoulder, and in practice lost the opportunity to influence the authorities' choice of policy. This has had an enormous impact, both on politics and the development of economics.

**The arguments for and against inflation**

We will take a closer look at the economists' discussions, and contrary to what has been the tradition in the public debate in the past 100 years, I am going to let the *critics* of inflation come to the fore. First, we look at the main arguments for and against inflation. Former governor of Norges Bank Øystein Olsen mentioned in his lecture *The Monetary Policy's objective and scope,* October 26, 2017, at BI Norwegian Business School the two postulates that are most used as an argument that inflation is good, when he said that "Some inflation can grease the gears of the economy, while at the same time increasing the room for maneuver in monetary policy."

In other words, the argument is twofold: firstly, that inflation is *good for the economy*, and secondly, that it is *good for politics*. Proponents of inflation often add that being able to adjust the growth of the money supply gives the state the opportunity to influence how much investment is made in society, for example in production capacity and innovation. They believe that the government can thus contribute to low unemployment. The theory is that creating new money encourages people to spend more and that this in turn encourages companies to invest and expand their workforce.

Opponents of inflation policy belong primarily to what we call the *Austrian School* of Economics. The difference between this and other schools or traditions concerning the approach to economic theory and economic method is also an important theme in this book. The reason is that this is where we find some of the explanation for the disagreement. The economists of the Austrian school believe that increasing the money supply does not give society anything positive, and that money cannot become more and more valuable to society, as long as the purchasing power of money is reduced for those who own it.

They also believe that the expansion of the money supply causes a *redistribution* of society's resources, from almost all the society on the one hand, to speculators, the rich and especially to the government on the other. Inflation functions as a straw from the person who uses the new money first, down into the pockets of those who accept the money as payment for goods and services. The Austrian economists point out that the more people who must use this type of money, the greater the overall redistribution effect, and the greater the value of the expansion of the money supply for those who use the money in the early stages of transactions.

Opponents also argue that inflation leads to harmful market fluctuations, speculation, that real estate, labor, and capital are being pulled away from the production of goods and services that are important to us, and that ever greater resources end up in the hands of very few people.

Inflation also causes depopulation and centralization. The reason is that the influx of new money is greatest in the big cities, especially where the public sector and the financial industry have a large presence. The rural areas normally receive much less of the new money. This imbalance leads to higher price inflation in the cities than in the outskirts, making investments in real estate and capital more profitable in the cities, compared to the outskirts. Thus, inflation functions as a catalyst on the flow of capital and labor, from the least populated areas and into the most populated areas.

**The real economy and the financial economy**

In a modern economy, there is a close interaction between what we call *the real economy* and *the financial economy*.

The real economy includes society's real values, i.e., non-financial values. We traditionally divide real values into three categories of scarce resources: real estate, labor, and capital.

The financial economy includes money and securities that are claims to money, as well as securities that are claims to and rights to real values.

The financial economy has emerged from the real economy because of trade. The main function of the financial economy is to facilitate the transfer of claims to real values so that scarce resources can contribute in the best possible way to meeting the needs of the people. The ability of the financial economy to contribute to this depends largely on the quality of money and the monetary system. With what we call "unsound money", the financial economy will primarily contribute to the redistribution of real values, at the expense of meeting the needs of the public.

**The 12 zeros**

Inflation forces us to talk about big numbers. A trillion has 12 zeros, which is the same as a thousand billion.

**The money's journey, status today and political measures**

When we have reviewed historical developments and the debate among economists, we take a closer look at the current monetary system. We start with the central banks and discuss who owns and controls them. We will also look at what happens from the moment new money is created, and as it begins to circulate through society, with one transaction superseding the other, up to the nadir after the market crash that money printing always leads to. In that chapter, we pick up the thread from the chapter on the history of inflation as a policy and interweave it with the journey of money until we arrive at today's situation. Following on from that, we take stock of the current economic situation where we emphasize how wealth has been distributed, before looking at how politicians relate to the question of how to solve the problem with inflation.

**Concluding chapters**

The last part of the book begins with a discussion on how the system affects society leading to what sort of changes we can expect in the future. Towards the end, we take a look at saving and investment in an economy plagued with inflation, some reasons for being optimistic and some ideas on how one can handle inflation as an individual.

**The lesson**

The most important lesson you will learn from this book is that:

- Unlike other financial resources, the total value of fiat money in circulation does not increase when the supply of fiat money increases

- The longer time passes while the supply of fiat money increases, and the faster it grows, the less freedom we are left with, and the greater the redistribution of wealth becomes

- It is possible for both citizens and states to opt out of the inflation economy – in whole or in part

- There will be great advantages to abolishing states' monopolies on money and re-establishing monetary freedom

# The history of inflation as a policy

**Introduction**

In this chapter, we review important developments in the history of inflation policy. The goal is to build a basic understanding of where the ideas behind today's government control of money, what is called *monetary policy*, come from, and the power and room for maneuver that the state gains through monetary policy.

When the city-state of Athens fought the Peloponnesian War against Sparta almost 2,500 years ago, from 431 BCE to 414 BCE, they financed the war with a combination of money inflation and taxation. The Athenians created money inflation by reducing the amount of gold and silver in the coins they used so that they could produce more coins. They lost the war, Athens ran into great financial trouble, and in 404 BCE they surrendered to Sparta. Almost 2,000 years ago, the emperors of the Roman Empire also systemized inflation whilst expanding the empire and further bolstering state power. The policy contributed to major economic and social problems that eventually led to the dissolution of the Roman Empire as it was split down the middle. The Western Roman Empire collapsed in 476 CE, while the Eastern Roman Empire persisted until 1453 CE.

The Chinese were early adopters of paper money. As early as 1020 CE, extensive monetary inflation has been reported due to banknote production during the S'ung dynasty, and in 1166 CE it is said to have been hyperinflation during the Chin Dynasty. When Marco Polo returned to Europe in 1296 CE and told people about the monetary system that he had seen in China, they found it hard to believe that he was telling the truth.

Many have written about inflation in Athens, the Roman Empire and in the various dynasties in China and what the policy led to. I have chosen to start with the Viking Age and the Vikings' monetary system. A lot has been written about coin production in the Viking Age, but with respect to the monetary policy it has largely faded into history. The chapter concentrates on the almost 1,000-year period from when Harald Hardråde first took power towards the end of the Viking Age and up to the present day.

Among other things, we look at the establishment of the world's first central bank, which has its origin in Sweden, and how and why this spread to other countries. Finally, we look at the introduction of what is called the *gold standard*, its repeal, and indeed how the introduction of two successive international agreements on a *gold exchange standard* and the repeal of these led to the fiat monetary system that we have all over the world today. We also look at the emergence and growing prominence of cryptocurrency.

We review historical developments relatively thoroughly, before looking at the discussion between economists in the next chapter. The story of how the concept of inflation arose and how it was further developed as a political tool contains within most of what one needs to understand what this is all about. It is hoped that you will also understand more about which theoretical and ethical arguments may be valid and which may carry the greatest weight. It is further hoped that you will then be able to sift away or parse those arguments that are invalid, carry less weight, that only serve to muddy the waters, or those elements that make it all the more difficult to keep your eyes fixed on what really matters: **the big picture.**

**The monetary system in the Viking age**

The Viking Age in Northern Europe lasted from about 760 AD to 1066 AD. The Norwegians used coins as a means of payment. King Olav Tryggvason is the first Norwegian king who we know began minting coins, in 995. Historians believe that he didn't start any major coin production. Archaeological finds indicate that for most of the Viking Age we were free to use the coins that we liked best. The Vikings preferred coins that were known for high and stable elements of valuable metal, primarily silver, and used a lot of coins from abroad.

Sometime before the year 995, Åsta Gudbrandsdatter married Harald Grenske, and they had a son named Olav Haraldsson. Harald died and Åsta remarried Sigurd Syr, and they had a son named Harald Sigurdsson. According to the sagas, both Olav Haraldsson and his half-brother Harald Sigurdsson were descendants of Harald Fairhair, who united the petty kingdoms in Norway into one around 885.

In my home county of Trøndelag in central Norway we had a law at that time, called the *Frostating law*. The law had the following warning: "By law the land shall be built, and by unlaw it shall be destroyed." It also had some special "resistance provisions" that did not exist in other Nordic laws. It stated:

> No man shall do tilferd* to a man, neither the King nor any other man. But if the King does so, an army arrow [war messenger] shall be cut. It shall go in all eight counties, and all the peasants shall go against the King and kill him if they can. But if the King escapes, he shall never be allowed to return to the country. Whoever will not go against him shall make three marks, and likewise the one who does not pass on the arrow.

«Tilferd*» was the same as someone taking someone else's property without the consent of the Frostating (the parliament in Trøndelag). The provision set up a principle of separation of powers aimed at protecting the people of Trøndelag against dictatorial royal power. Violation of the law led to harsher punishment for the king than for others. The law entailed both the *right and the duty* of the

Trønders (residents of Trøndelag) to kill the King if he took people's property, for example by imposing taxes, if it was not previously approved by the Frostating.

Olav Haraldsson became King of Norway in 1015. He ruled the country with a heavy hand and confiscated a great deal of property. He made many enemies and lost a lot of political power, and in 1028, the Trønders drove him out of the country with the support of King Knut of Denmark. The incident has therefore been seen by historians both in the context of the resistance provisions of the Frostating Act and the power struggle between the Danish and Norwegian Royal Families.

Olav wanted to reclaim his power in Norway. In 1030, he and his half-brother Harald took an army through Sweden and into Verdalen in Trøndelag. The Trønders were well prepared, and with the support of King Knut, they had gathered a large army waiting for Olav and his men at Stiklestad. The Trønders won, and Olav died in the battle. Later he became known as St. Olav. His half-brother Harald was injured and fled the country. Eventually he wound his way to Constantinople, what the Vikings called Miklagard, today known as Istanbul, Turkey. Miklagard was at that time the capital of the powerful Byzantine Empire, synonymously known as the Eastern Roman Empire. Harald and his men served in the emperor's national guard.

In Constantinople, Harald saw that those in power had abolished the freedom of money. Instead, they had developed a mint and introduced a monetary monopoly which meant that the people were not allowed to use coins other than those that were "struck", that is, minted, by the state apparatus, bearing an official mark. He learned that the money monopoly was an important source of income for the rulers of the Eastern Roman Empire.

Harald eventually returned to Norway, and in the year 1046 he became King. In 1050 Harald plotted against the powerful Trønder, Earl Einar Tambarskjelve, and killed both he and his son Eindride. The murder took place in Nidaros, which today is called Trondheim, and which is the largest city in Trøndelag. This dealt a severe blow to the position of the people of Trøndelag, while at the same time gave Harald increased political room for maneuver.

That same year, Harald set up his own mint in Nidaros. He decided that everyone had to accept his coins. Violation of the law was punishable by death. This policy led to Harald's coins having an *artificially high value* compared to other coins. Harald ruled the country in the same heavy-handed manner as Olav, and this is the reason why he was nicknamed *Hardråde* ("hard ruler").

Those who wanted exchangeable money had to hand over silver so that it may be melted and minted. Harald also set up a mint in Hamar, which developed into one of the larger cities in Eastern Norway. The geography of the mints was not accidental. The royal power was weakest in Trøndelag and eastern Norway, and in Constantinople he had probably seen how important a function the cities had in building up and retaining their power. Harald also built royal estates in the cities. He is also considered the founder of Oslo, today's capital of Norway. We will return to the relationship between inflation and centralization at a later stage.

The completed coins people were supplied with from Harald's mints had a lower content of silver than the coins they had handed over. He thus kept a share of the silver that the people handed in. This practice is today called "seigniorage," which means the net income that someone gets when they issue money.

The mint replaced silver with other lower-value metals. In this way, Harald reduced the silver content of the coins over time, from 90% to 33%. Harald minted new coins with the surplus silver and could use these for whatever he wanted. In this way, he also increased the number of coins in society, which means that he expanded the money supply.

The principal reason why Harald chose this strategy over any other probably lies with the following: Firstly, he had great ambitions for what he wanted to accomplish as King, ambitions that he had to finance in some way. Secondly, the Frostating Act's resistance provisions made it difficult for him to obtain funding via taxes and fees. If he was to avoid suffering the same fate as Olav, he was dependent on getting the Frostating to accept a tax increase. It can't have been easy, considering that the Trønders were a stubborn people, who would not contribute to the growth of royal power. They had seen the consequences for them, and Harald must have understood a little of their thought process. Finally, increasing the money supply by exploiting the money monopoly encouraged the possibility that he could achieve the same without imposing high taxes, and hopefully without the Trønders accusing him of having committed a direct violation of the Frostating Act.

By choosing monetary inflation, it would also prove more difficult for people to notice that the royal power was gradually acquiring more and more wealth at the expense of everyone else. He used his revenues from the money monopoly in the same way as he used revenues from taxes, for his own consumption, salaries to the soldiers, arms purchases, war financing and so on.

Harald's laws meant that the coins he minted were artificially high in value as a means of payment compared to other coins with a similar silver content. At the same time, this meant that foreign coins were of similarly artificially, low value. Historians believe that almost all foreign coinage had disappeared from circulation in Norway when Harald died. Probably a lot of silver coins disappeared to countries that had monetary freedom. There they could be used without anyone confiscating a share of the silver, which meant that they had greater value in those places than in Norway. This phenomenon is called *Gresham's Law*, which states that "bad money drives out good money".

Logically it follows that the consequence of Harald's policy was, more than likely, the country was gradually drained of silver, which was a great loss for society. In today's parlance, an economist would say that it has "weakened our international purchasing power." It shows how few people benefit from inflation, and how much society at large loses from it.

If the King is to prevent the drainage of silver, inflation policy must be combined with a ban on exporting it out of the country. This means more coercion and what we today call "export control", which may require further development of the state apparatus. Harald presumably solved this problem by taking the soldiers abroad to pillage more silver.

But now we come to the most important points:

By reducing the silver in the coins from, for example, 90% to 45%, Harald was able to double the money supply. This doubling means that the value of each coin would be halved. What that means in practice is that, on average, people would have to spend twice as many coins to buy the same goods and services.

The revenue from the silver mint also enabled Harald to acquire both labor and other scarce resources to a greater extent. These resources then had to be *redistributed*, i.e., they were wrenched away from ordinary people and ended up in Harald's coffers.

Assuming that it took time for the people to discover that the silver content had decreased, the first to receive coins as payment when they sold something to Harald would be the ones who lost the least. Like Harald, they could then use the newly minted coins themselves to buy goods and services at "yesterday's" price.

As time passed, more and more people would discover that the silver content was lower, and that coins were more abundant. People would start demanding more coins to compensate for the fact that they had less silver. Since they also got more money through their hands, they would also start to accept that they would have to pay a higher price.

Those who received the new money long after Harald had used it to buy what he needed, had to struggle the most with the rise in prices. The result was that Harald and the first to receive the money from him, gained at the expense of everyone else. In reality, scarce resources and the value of labor were gradually transferred from everyone else to those who were allowed to spend the new money at the earliest, i.e., primarily to Harald. It is those who receive the money last who run the greatest risk of losing out on this. It will be easier to see this mechanism when we deal with paper money later on.

For the person who sits at the top and controls inflation and spends the new money first, the effect will be greatest the more people that he can convince or force to use his coins. If, for example, Harald had managed to force large parts of Europe to use his coins, it would have been as if a straw went from Harald's headquarters in Norway and out into every single country in Europe. There would have been a flow of newly minted coins from Harald into Europe, and a corresponding flow of real values back to him. What Norway would be left with would largely depend on which goods and services Harald preferred to buy.

Economists also call the redistributive effect the "inflation tax." Inflation also has the same effect in our time, even though we no longer use silver coins.

The challenge for Harald was that people could detect inflation directly, simply by virtue of being a sentient human being. For example, freshly minted coins with a high silver content will be shinier, heavier, softer and have a different sound than if the coin consists of, say, iron or copper, which are metals that are imbued of a much lower value. If Harald was to succeed in securing the inflation tax, he would therefore have to reduce the silver content gradually over time. If he did not proceed carefully, he risked the discovery that the coins contained less silver, therefore running the risk that the people demand to receive more coins in payment.

The royal saga about Harald Hardråde tells us that the Icelandic Halldor Snorrason, who was one of Harald's elite soldiers and member of his royal guard, saw through Harald, when Harald was to pay what they called "the sold", i.e., salary. Halldor had accompanied Harald to Miklagard and was one of those upon whom Harald was most dependent on his unmitigated loyalty. We can assume that Harald and Halldor had previously agreed that Halldor would receive a certain number of silver coins, or silver coins that had a certain total weight, as a salary for the services that he performed for Harald. The saga says:

> Eight days after Christmas, the men were paid sold. That payment was called Haraldsslåtten and mostly consisted of copper, at the best half silver. When Halldor got his sold, he poured them into a tab of his cloak and looked at them. The silver did not seem particularly good. Then he struck with his other hand so that money fell into the hay.

What probably happened was that Harald used coins that came directly from the mint, and that they possessed a lower silver content than Halldor understood to be the norm, which was the basis for the agreement they had made regarding wages. Halldor understood what had happened right away. We can imagine that he thought about the problems that he and the other soldiers would face when buying goods and services from traders and others. It would end in quarrels, use of force and ultimately would lead to them having to pay a greater amount of money for the goods bought, compared with previous purchases. Harald's inflation was a breach of contract on his part, and the soldiers were in danger of bestowing some of the value of their labor as a kind-of-gift to him. Halldor understood *the redistribution effect* intuitively.

He saw what Harald did for what it really was: A fraud. Halldor also knew that Harald had many enemies, and that the King was completely dependent on making amends for the loyalty that Halldor had shown him. Instead of being furious, he calmly rejected the bad *Haraldsslåtten* and let the coins fall into the hay. This episode also illustrates how far a King may be willing to go to increase his wealth at the expense of his subjects. But how could Harald take such a low-yield, high-impact risk? Afterall, we are talking about an elite soldier to whom he entrusted his life.

The answer is that, possibly, Harald needed an efficient means of getting the newly minted silver coins into circulation. He needed society's acceptance that they were just as good a means of payment as the coins that were already in circulation. Then he had to use them to additionally cover his greatest expenses, and the payment of salaries to the soldiers was probably a prime example of that. Moreover, he knew that the secret could not be revealed: that he had reduced the silver content of the coins. If he were honest with the soldiers, compensating them by paying with more coins, it would in effect have been like "broadcasting" to the rest of the country that he was about to carry out another fraud. It follows then that everyone who wanted payment from him for goods and services would only require him to pay with more coins than before. This would give Harald zero revenue from inflation tax. It is part of the story that Halldor broke with Harald as early as 1051, i.e., the year after Harald began his inflation experiment with the Norwegian society, and that he returned home to Iceland.

This story teaches us first and foremost how crucial it is for a state power to succeed with an inflation policy, that it does so incrementally, slowly and almost imperceptibly, so that society tolerates it and as few people as possible uncover the ruse and rebel. In Trøndelag, Harald was also dependent on taxing the population by stealth, as the Frostating Act's resistance provisions stood in his way. The story also shows that the King had to deceive his closest allies if he were to succeed in his inflation policy.

Today, the levers of power operate a little differently. If the state is unwilling to share the inflation tax with others who have financial power, the politicians and the civil servants will quickly lose the support it needs to retain its political power. Today the state achieves this by allowing the money supply to grow through bank lending. On paper, the current monetary system looks almost democratic. It seems that it gives everyone an equal opportunity to secure a piece of the inflation tax, by allowing everyone who increases their debt to be the first user of newly created money. What few people understand is that it is those who get to take out the most loans who benefit from this, and that the vast majority of borrowers therefore nevertheless end up as losers. Over time, citizens become dependent on taking out ever-higher loans, almost as an alcoholic becomes more and more dependent on liquor. In the end, only a small, wealthy elite benefits from the inflation policy, in addition to the state.

If we now return to Harald, his thirst for power was, inexplicably, even greater than Olav's. The supply of income from taxes, conquests and inflation enabled him to build up a large military and political power.

Harald's ambitions grew, and eventually he realized that he wanted to conquer England. In 1066, he sailed out of Norway with a fleet consisting of more than 200 ships and somewhere between 7,000 - 9,000 soldiers. On 25th September, the English King Harold Godwinson and his men surprised Harald and the soldiers, who had camped near Stamford Bridge. Harald was felled and subsequently killed by an arrow that struck him in the throat. His soldiers met a similarly brutal and bloody end and were themselves summarily slaughtered on the battlefield. Thus, an era in Norway's inflation history was over.

Harald Hardråde's ambitions, his inflation policy and his waging of foreign warfare had major consequences. The attempt to take England is considered the last major Viking expedition, and it is fair to say that this also precipitated the end of the Viking Age.

In other words, history shows how strong a political instrument inflation can be. This can strengthen the state's power, but it can also contribute to that power spiraling out of control, not to mention widespread societal fluxes. It can hardly be a coincidence that the Viking Age ended with Harald and the Battle of Stamford Bridge. War comes at a cost and not managing to subjugate England was perhaps a greater cost, financially and spiritually, than the Viking culture was able to bear. The story of Harald is reflective of the fall of Ancient Athens and its loss to Sparta.

Harald's demise, however, did not mean that the Kings gave up using inflation as an instrument, quite the contrary. His son Olav Kyrre took over the royal seat of power in Norway. He also struck coin, both with high and low silver content. Olav Kyrre probably did as other regents did, starting with coins with a high silver content, gradually reducing that content incrementally.

The relationship between inflation and war is something we will return to several times when we follow the further development of inflation policy. We will then see that the combination of inflation, the transition to paper money and the establishment of a state-controlled banking systems that can provide loans to the state expands the possibilities of the Crown to finance warfare by expanding the money supply.

In summary, there were nine essential aspects of Harald Hardråde's monetary policy:

(1) The killing of political opponents
(2) Establishment of mints in cities and regions where the king had the least power
(3) A monetary monopoly that gave the coins an artificially high value
(4) A debasement of the coins over time
(5) A redistribution of resources
(6) Enormous revenues to the king
(7) Ever-growing military ambitions
(8) A collapse following a bloody battle in which the King died
(9) The end of the Viking age

In addition, we have noted that coins with a high silver content probably disappeared out of the country, as Gresham's Law dictates. We can also then consider that a reduction in silver from 90 to 33% over the course of 16 years means that Harald tripled the money supply. It is uncertain how deliberately and gradually he reduced the silver content, but the average increase in the money supply during these years amounted to about 7%, per year.

**Revolution and reintroduction of monetary freedom in the Netherlands**

The inflation policy of the Eastern Roman Empire spread, and gradually all Kings of Europe introduced such laws as those Harald Hardråde had imposed upon Trøndelag and the rest of the Norway in 1050. Charles V, Emperor of the Holy Roman Empire from 1519 to 1556, who ruled the Netherlands from 1505 to 1555, was a notorious inflationist. The people carried the burden, and following Gresham's law, coins of high value disappeared from the kingdom. King Philip II of Spain took over the rule of the Netherlands, but in 1566 the Dutch revolted and freed themselves from tyranny.

One of the first things that the revolutionaries did was to abolish the inflation policy and decide that everyone was free to use whatever coins they wanted. In the article *The Dutch Monetary Environment During Tulipmania,* Douglas E. French, an Austrian school economist, writes that the revolutionaries derived the idea of freedom of money from the Dutch colony in Eastern India. The Dutch took over the colony from the Portuguese. The practice of monetary freedom could be traced via a region in today's Portugal, and to a part of today's India during the 7th century AD, which at that time was under Muslim rule.

The Dutch had their own mints where everyone could hand over coins to be melted down and minted into coins they called *guilders*, for a small fee to cover the costs. This ensured the *recognition and standardization* of coins that people trusted to have the same stable content of valuable metal.

Monetary freedom laid a sound foundation for trade. In Europe, many people were left with gold and silver after *The Conquistadors'* many expeditionary raids to America. Many of them kept their fortunes hidden from the Kings, as well as their monetary monopoly. When the Netherlands changed its laws, it was as if the floodgates opened, spewing gold and silver into the country. The liberal coin laws helped the Netherlands become a leading trading nation, and by the 17th century the small nation had become one of the world's richest countries. They also gradually developed an advanced and profitable banking system, which attracted many customers from other countries. Customers deposited their money for safekeeping at the Bank of Amsterdam, which made a profit by keeping them secure and by taking fees for facilitating transactions between account holders.

The bank weighed and assessed the coins and gave customers notes which functioned as a proof of the value of the gold and silver in the coins they deposited. Customers gradually began to use the notes as a means of payment, instead of carrying coins. The value of banknotes changed in step with the value of silver and gold.

The Dutch were also major producers of tulips. They cultivated many beautiful species, some with advanced patterns, which were traded as luxury items. A significant export market also developed. From June, so-called *futures contracts* could be drawn up, which were agreements for the purchase of the following year's crop of tulips.

In the period 1633 to 1638, a lot of coins flowed in from other countries, and deposits in the Amsterdam Bank increased by 60%, from 5 million to 8 million *guilders*. This led to a general rise in prices, and additionally, some of the money found its way to the tulip futures market. Speculation flourished and gradually people from all walks of life threw themselves wholeheartedly into the craze. Information about the trade is characterized by some uncertain source material, and while some claim that in 1635 a futures contract was signed for a future supply of 40 tulip bulbs at a price of 100,000 guilders, others claim that this has been greatly exaggerated. Anne Goldgar, a professor at King's College London, writes in her book *Tulipmania: Money, Honor and Knowledge in the Dutch Golden Age* that she found evidence that 37 people paid more than 300 guilders for one bulb. By any measure, that is a high price to pay, when compared with the annual salary of a skilled worker which at that time was between 150 and 350 guilders.

The publisher says about French's 1992 book *Early Speculative Bubbles and Increases in the Supply of Money* that:

> Tulipmania was unique in that it was the sound money policy of the Dutch combined with free coinage laws that led to an acute increase in the supply of money and fostered an atmosphere that was ripe for speculation and manifesting itself in the intense trading of tulip bulbs.

The bubble burst when it proved impossible to sell a batch of tulip bulbs at an auction on February 3rd, 1637. Afterwards, prices plummeted, and there were many disputes about whether the contracting parties could demand settlement in accordance with the contracts they had made. On the basis that the government had banned gambling, the courts decided that some of the agreements were invalid. Goldgar writes that only a small group of people lost money and that the incident did not trigger an economic crisis for the Netherlands.

The tulip bubble occurred as a result of other countries having laws and regulations that led to some money achieving artificially high value, while other money had artificially low value. This illustrates that the value of money other than fiat money also decreases when it accumulates within a geographically delineated area.

However, the two most important lessons from the Dutch Tulip bubble are:

(1) A rapid expansion of the money supply leads to extensive speculation and that many lose ground, and
(2) A speculation bubble in an economy with sound money does not have to inflict major societal damage.

Goldgar mentions that many of those who were wealthy reacted negatively to having to associate with newly rich people who came from lower echelons of society, who enjoyed rapid success without having to work hard for it.

The Bank of Amsterdam initially offered no credit, that is, it did not engage in lending activities. In 1657, someone discovered that the bank had allowed customers to overdraw their accounts, i.e., they issued notes that exceeded the value of the coins that the customers had deposited. Practically, this meant that the bank provided credit without 100% reserves. This developed into a practice that contributed to a new upsurge in speculation in the markets of the Netherlands. In parallel with this, the country's position as a great power began to weaken. In 1790 it became known that the bank had given large loans to the Dutch

East India Company, the bank subsequently filed for bankruptcy and the following year it was nationalized. The supremacy of the Dutch guilder was over, and the English *pound sterling* became the new dominant currency in most of the world.

**Stockholm Banco, Sweden – the forerunner of the first central bank**

Johan Palmstruch was born in 1611 in Riga, Latvia. He was the son of a Dutch merchant. In 1635, amid the tulip speculation, he became a citizen of Amsterdam. Palmstruch moved to Stockholm in 1647 and was knighted in 1651. In 1656, he received a license from the King of Sweden, Charles X which allowed him set up a bank, named *Stockholm Banco*. In return, the King demanded payment in the form of a share of the profits.

At this time, it was primarily copper that was used as money in Sweden. The reason was that Sweden was one of the largest producers of copper. The king's mint struck copper coins, just as Harald Hardråde's mint had struck silver coins.

Stockholm Banco opened in 1657. A high-ranking civil servant named Seved Bååth deposited a large deposit in the form of a copper coin. We can imagine that the confidence in the bank among the people grew when they heard that a man of such standing deposited so much money there. Eventually, many people followed suit and did the same as Bååth.

The customers were given a receipt for the deposit. If the customer wanted to transfer part of the deposit to someone else, the transaction had to be noted in the bank, so that the money was transferred from one account to the other. The bank was obliged to hand out the deposit at the owner's request. Palmstruch also offered loans on the condition that the borrower could deposit silver or gold as collateral. The customers who accepted the lending of their coins were paid in the form of interest. The bank's profit corresponded to the difference between lending rates and deposit rates.

In 1660, King Charles X died. The Secretary of State temporarily took control and decided that people had to remint their coins. The motive was the same as Harald Hardråde's: that the state should earn revenue in the form of *seigniorage*. The decision became public knowledge. Those who had deposits in Stockholm Banco begun to fear that they would be handed coins with a low copper content, which they knew would surely be possessed of a lower value in the purchase of goods and services than the money that they had originally deposited in the bank. They understood that this would mean that they would have to pay higher prices and that they were the ones who would lose out. It was obvious that it was the government, and perhaps also the bank, which would get all the benefits.

The news led to a "run on the bank". Customers wanted to withdraw their copper coins while it was still possible to get coins that had the same high proportion of copper as before, so that they would not suffer losses. Because the bank had started lending deposits, it didn't have the same number of coins available that its owners had deposited. Thus, the bank ran out of coins as more people came to withdraw their deposits. It also meant that people didn't want to deposit more money in the bank. At the same time, people had become accustomed to the fact that they could borrow money, so the demand for loans was still there. Palmstruch offered people higher interest rates to deposit money, money which the bank could lend to others, but people were inevitably suspicious and the bank's coin shortage situation remained precarious.

Palmstruch was familiar with a practice that had taken root in connection with a company called Stora Kopparberg's and their mining activities. When the miners handed in copper for weighing in, they received receipts showing how much copper the company had received. The receipts were proof of how much the workers were entitled to on payday. Regardless of how this was connected, they had implemented a practice where the workers used the receipts as a means of payment for goods and services, that is, the receipts circulated in the local community as money, on a par with coins.

For this to work, the mining company must have accepted that the person or entity that had obtained receipts, could demand settlement from the company in the form of copper. The reality was that those who accepted the receipts as payment provided credit to the workers until payday.

On Stora Kopparberg's part, the only potential drawback was that they increased the risk that they could be exposed to fraud by someone falsifying the receipts. By keeping tight accounts and punishing fraud harshly, they could take steps to limit the risk of fraudulent activity taking place.

The system carried with it obvious advantages for the company. The employees presumably became quickly dependent on the scheme, insofar as they could spend their wages in advance. If the workers demanded more in wages, the company could therefore threaten to abolish the practice of allowing people other than the workers to redeem the receipts for copper coins. This could therefore help the company to keep wages down.

The system gave Palmstruch the idea that he could issue banknotes to those who had deposited coins in the bank. The notes were to state that the holder, i.e., the person holding the notes, was entitled to demand that the bank pay a given number of coins. In other words, without the bank having to seek approval of the transfer from the customer who had originally deposited the money nor the person who was to take over the note.

Palmstruch understood that people needed to have confidence that the bank would settle on demand, when they came to redeem their banknotes in copper coins. If people did not trust that the notes had lasting value as money, they would be reluctant to accept it as payment moving forward. Palmstruch therefore persuaded the finance minister to decide that the people could use the banknotes to pay taxes and duties. Thus, the *first* of three important components, *trust*, was in place.

Banknotes began to circulate in Sweden from 1661. People quickly became accustomed to the fact that they could just as easily use banknotes as coins when paying for goods and services. Eventually, Palmstruch introduced a new lending practice, this being the *second* important component: the bank began to issue loans in the form of banknotes, in return for customers paying interest to the bank. In principle, such a practice should not be a disadvantage to anyone, *as long as* the bank kept reserves in the form of copper coins that amounted to the same value as the banknotes represented.

The problem was that Palmstruch was tempted to issue banknotes when people took out loans *without* increasing the value of the bank's coin reserves accordingly. This was the *third* important component. This innovation in the banking industry is called "fractional reserve banking". In principle, this was the same thing as what the Amsterdam Bank did a few years earlier, when it allowed people to overdraft their accounts.

Stockholm Banco began issuing more and more loans. The King also took out loans on behalf of the state. One may ask how people reacted when they learned the king was taking out loans. Did they think the same as when civil servant Bååth made his deposits in the bank, that the king's borrowing indicated that it was both a safe bet and a smart move? Did anyone start pondering whether it still made sense to deposit copper coins in the bank? Were they thinking that there was a risk that the bank would not have enough coins if everyone came running with their notes, and whether or not the bank would prioritize the King over everyone else if it had too few?

Whatever people may have thought, it remains a fact that the demand for loans and banknotes from Stockholm Banco increased quickly. Banknotes entered circulation in increasingly large areas and were gradually used as a means of payment in many major European cities. The bank certainly received high revenues while this practice was going on, and it is likely that others also gained a lot by taking advantage of the opportunities that an influx of new money offered.

Gradually, people became aware that banknotes began to circulate as a means of payment on a very large scale. Thus, they also understood that Palmstruch must have printed an enormous number of banknotes. And if he had, he would have had to receive a similarly enormous amount of copper in an equally short time. That is to say – if he were to be able to keep his promise if many wished to redeem their banknotes. But where did all this copper come from? Did the bank have such large amounts of coins that it could guarantee settlement for everyone who had banknotes?

Soon enough, anxiety amongst the people grew about whether the bank really had so much copper that it would be able to settle its accounts with everyone. In 1663, this ended with *bank run No. 2* against Stockholm Banco. People rushed to the bank's headquarters and branches to withdraw their deposits, while demanding to exchange all their notes for coins. Palmstruch, of course, didn't have nearly enough copper coin. In practice, he sat and administered a massive pyramid scheme that was doomed to end with a huge meltdown.

The news led to a loss of confidence in banknotes as a means of payment, thereby also reducing the value of the notes. This meant that those who wanted to pay for goods and services with banknotes had to pay with more and larger banknotes than they had done before. The bank went bankrupt, many were left with almost worthless banknotes and experienced great financial difficulties. Those who both held large quantities of banknotes while at the same time having entered into agreements in which they had assumed large payment obligations incurred the biggest losses. There is every reason to believe that many went bankrupt.

Palmstruch was sentenced to death in 1669, a sentence that was commuted to life imprisonment, further commuted to his release in 1670. He died the following year, ruined and in disgrace.

What remained was The State, who emerged as the big winner. It had probably made good money on its share of profits while the lending business flourished. In addition, the government had taken the opportunity to take out huge loans, and it had most probably spent most of the banknotes. Whereupon the fraud was uncovered, the banknotes were almost worthless. We can assume that the borrowers were not obliged to repay the loans with anything other than banknotes and that the debtors could buy banknotes at a great discount in the market.

What is clear is that Palmstruch was hung out to dry, made a scapegoat, while the King probably got away with just a few proverbial cuts and bruises in what was perhaps already a blemished reputation. When the government itself is complicit in fraud, there is little that society can do.

The inflation scheme that the state and Stockholm Banco had jointly set up was based upon:

(1) Trust
(2) Expansion of the money supply without increasing reserves accordingly
(3) Large government borrowings
(4) No negative consequences for the government
(5) The banker Palmstruch plays the role of capitalist scapegoat
(6) The government has all the advantages

This would become the recipe for modern monetary policy. It would also have enormous consequences for the development of society right into our own time.

**Riksens Ständers Bank of Sweden – the world's first central bank**

News of Stockholm Banco's hefty story spread throughout Europe. Nevertheless, it was some other Swedes who were the first to look at the possibility of doing something similar. Inspired by Palmstruch, the Swedish nobility took the initiative in as early as 1668 to set up what would eventually become the World's first central bank, Riksens Ständers Bank. As part of the ongoing power struggle with the nobility, King Charles XI decided that he would take control of the bank.

The National Bank was given the authority to decide the value of money and the size of the money supply. The King also allowed the establishment of private commercial banks. These banks could issue their own banknotes, if they deposited reserves with the national bank, as a guarantee of the notes that banks issued to their loan customers. In addition, the national bank itself also issued banknotes. This meant that Sweden set up the world's first central bank, and that the Swedes received the pyramid that we talked about in the introduction.

His son king Charles XII would prove to be one of Europe's most warmongering Kings. In the period up to 1718, he took out large loans from the central bank to finance warfare in the Nordic countries, and in Eastern Europe, including countries such as Russia and Poland.

Like Stockholm Banco, the central bank began issuing significantly larger loans than it had copper reserves to settle if everyone returned to exchange their notes for copper coins. The King himself had control of the bank, and if society had confidence that the money could be used to pay taxes and fees along with everything else that had to be paid, this arrangement did not entail any appreciable risk to him and his rule. However, he took more and more risk in his waging of wars, and needed more and more money. The bank responded by printing banknotes, which it loaned to the King.

Like the first of the two *bank runs* against Stockholm Banco, there was one particular incident that caused confidence in the money to suddenly disappear. In one of Charles' many campaigns, he suffered a massive defeat in 1709 at the Ukrainian city of Poltava. When the news reached Sweden, people panicked, and a new *bank run* was set in motion. The banks copper reserves were insufficient, the value of the bank notes depreciated, the state's treasury was empty, and the Swedes were plunged into an economic crisis. The bank continued to run, but it took decades for the banknote owners to regain their assets.

Charles XII did not lose heart. His adviser, Georg Heinrich von Görtz, suggested that they produce "emergency coins" in copper, which the holder could exchange for silver when the King's military campaigns were over. In the period 1715 to 1719, the mint struck more than 40 million "emergency dalers", creating a price inflation of almost 50% and a further deterioration in the Swedish people's situation. The King was killed in Halden in 1718, when he invaded Norway. There are several historians who believe that he was shot by one of his own men, as his troops were tired of his wars and his system of government. Görtz was blamed for the economic problems suffered by the Swedes. He was sentenced to death and on February 19th, 1719, he was executed.

This story shows that the combination of paper money and a state-owned central bank made it even easier to finance warfare with inflation. It also confirms the experience from Harald Hardråde's time, that inflation is a strong political instrument that can cascade out of control, in such a way that kings take too much risk with their country, not to mention their own lives. Furthermore, we see yet another example of finding a scapegoat who takes attention away from the role of the government.

In addition to Palmstruch's innovations, the establishment of Riksens Ständers Bank and the structuring of the new monetary system meant that:

- More private banks could be incorporated
- The private banks were subject to the regulation of the Riksbank, including the value of money
- It became a requirement that the other banks deposit reserves for their loans with the Riksbank

Thus, not only was the national bank a useful bank for the King and those who took out loans, but it also became a central bank in the sense that it coordinated other private banks' contribution to the growth of the money supply. The greatest effect of becoming a regulatory central bank would only appear later.

One might think that the states would learn from the mistakes of the past, that they would begin to understand that inflation and war were connected like children of evil, that there is a danger that it will go to the heads of kings, inflating the sense of their own immortality, and that it ends badly for both King and country. But, alas, this was not to be the case.

**John Law deceives France**

John Law, baptized 21 April 1671 in Edinburgh, Scotland, was an economist, financier, banker, writer, and a gambler. He studied probability theory and so leveraged his knowledge to make big money from his gambling exploits. He preferred to take on the role of the game's *bank*, because the odds were normally more advantageous for the bank than for the other players. In other words: the house always wins.

In 1694, he was challenged to a pistols-at-dawn duel whereupon he prevailed and killed his opponent. Duels being as they were contrary to common law, he was sentenced to death, a punishment that was later commuted to prison time, before making good his escape to Amsterdam. Law, ever the industrious thinker, began to study banking. Presumably, he must have seen the speculative economy that developed in the wake of the Bank of Amsterdam's policy of issuing credit without having 100% reserves.

Law also began writing op-ed pieces and implemented several initiatives in order to make the heads of state in Europe think about changing their financial policies. He argued strongly for the use of paper money and so proposed creating a paper money economy, that economy being secured with reserves in the form of real estate, instead of the traditional method of securing against the value of gold. Nobody took his suggestions seriously.

King Louis XIV of France died in 1715. He had wrung out every last penny in his treasury in order to build himself an opulent palace at Versailles, not to mention his penchant for warmongering. The people of France were destitute. In anticipation of the rightful heir to the throne ascending, Philippe II, the Duke of Orleans, took over as interim regent. Law contacted the Duke, and he finally found a sympathetic ear, the Duke all-too-happy to entertain his theories. In 1716, Law succeeded in persuading the Regent to grant permission for the establishment of the Banque Générale. Law staked 25% of the equity, while the French Government covered the remaining 75%.

Initially, Law conducted his business in such a way that people began to gain confidence in the bank. The success created envy in their competitors, who deposited a large sum in Banque Générale, understanding that they could find holes in this new system. They waited until Law had loaned the deposits, before promptly returning demanding to withdraw their money. Law did not have enough reserves, inevitably leaving the Regent having to rescue the bank financially.

It is unclear whether Law knew about the history of Stockholm Banco and the agreement that Palmstruch made with the finance minister, but the similarities in both procedures are too many for it to be mere coincidence. To strengthen confidence in the bank, Law managed to persuade the Regent to deposit coins in exchange for large sums in banknotes. The coins were transported to the bank fully in view of the public in broad daylight. The regent was at pains to ensure that as many people as possible would see it. In 1717, Law prompted a decision by the Regent stating that taxes had to be paid with banknotes issued by the bank. Law then began printing banknotes on an industrial scale. In addition, he managed to convince people to invest in the Mississippi Company, a trading company that Law also controlled in cahoots with the State.

In 1719, he also persuaded the Regent to declare that gold and silver coins would be confiscated and that those who did not hand them in should be punished. It didn't stop there, as in 1720 he further persuaded the Regent to decree that banknotes should be legal and compulsory tender throughout France, except for small transactions that could be paid with coins. In other words, Law succeeded in his quest to engineer a chain of events that saw France doing the exact opposite of what made the Netherlands one of the richest countries in the World in turn ensuring that Amsterdam was the trading capital of Europe.

The bank willingly loaned freshly printed notes to those who wanted to buy shares in the Mississippi Company, which served as an instrument for channeling money inflation. Prices rose sharply and speculation in the shares developed apace until May 1720. By then, people had lost confidence in Law and his business. His dubious scheme collapsed. Thousands of people were ruined, a lynch mob gathered and rounded up the bad actors. Law was placed under house arrest, more than likely for his own safety. Seven months later, he left Paris. He was unceremoniously stopped at the border, the guards stripping him of the coins he had on him, in accordance with the legislation that John Law himself had arranged to put in place. By that time, the value of the French currency, *livres,* had depreciated to such an extent that there was no official exchange rate against the English Pound Sterling. This prompted Voltaire to formulate his famous law on paper money, that "all paper money returns to its intrinsic value, that is, zero." John Law died a poor man in Venice in 1729.

The incident is often referred to as the first financial bubble in the world. Retrospectively, this is also the aspect of the story that has received the most attention. More importantly it wasn't just stock prices that rose while Law was running the printing press at full tilt. The massive printing of banknotes and the ban on the use of other money meant that prices for real estate, consumer goods and raw materials skyrocketed. In some places, prices more than doubled in the short lifespan of Law's scheme. Wages increased, albeit at a slower pace compared to the rapid rise in prices. Law's massive fraud therefore hit an already hard-pressed French working class, whose real wages dropped drastically.

**The idea of central banks spreads throughout Europe**

What Charles XII of Sweden had done would have appeared to kings of other countries as "do the same or suffer invasion". If a small country such as Sweden could become so powerful with the usage of paper money, what could happen if one of the big countries followed suit? Moreover, the system made it possible for speculators and others to profit from such a scheme. Similar monetary and banking systems therefore spread to many other Western countries. Many of the projects became short-lived affairs with state banks that quickly entered bankruptcy.

In the 17th and the 18th century, Norway was under Danish rule. This did not discourage high-spirited Norwegians who understood the benefits of such a monetary system. According to Nicolai Rygg's book *Norges Bank's History*, Vol.1, many private individuals proposed the establishment of a Norwegian Central Bank in the 1700s. For example, in 1770 a group of "citizens of Kristiania and Drammen" sent an application to the Danish King, imploring him to set up a fund of 500,000 *riksdaler*, for the establishment of a National Bank. They proposed that it should be allowed to print banknotes for a total of triple its value, i.e., 1,500,000 riksdaler. The banknotes were to be made available as loans to the private sector. The authors of the letter argued that this would produce lower interest rates, better prices for export goods and lower prices for imported goods. The Danish King was certainly aware of what had happened in Sweden and France 50 years earlier. He further understood very well the role the Norwegians could play. Afterall, it was they who had written the letter in the first place. Unsurprisingly perhaps, the initiative was a failure.

The first Central Bank in Norway did not come into being until 1816, two years after Denmark's dominion over Norway had ceased. However, the central bank, named Norges Bank, was not allowed to extend loans directly to the government.

The Bank of England was founded in 1694, then as a private bank. Russia created its central bank in 1860 and Germany in 1875. The vast majority of European governments had gradually established their own central banks.

There are two points that are worth noting with this development:

(1) The introduction of central bank models would help coordination of monetary policy across national borders
(2) An increased risk for the government to lose control of the monetary policy to other states and to the financial elite

**The era of the gold standard**

The Bank of England adopted what is known as the "gold standard" in 1718. It stated that 4.25 Pounds Sterling was equivalent to one ounce of gold. This meant that those who had banknotes could go to the bank and demand redemption of the banknotes in gold. This contributed to the Pound taking over the Dutch Guilders' role as the world's reserve currency. The British passed the gold standard into law in 1816. Several other countries followed suit.

If banks loaned too much money, thereby expanding the number of notes in circulation to an excessive degree, banks would risk new *banking runs*. To avoid this, the central banks had the authority to regulate the lending activities of other banks. If the money supply increased too much, the central bank counteracted this by raising interest rates, which reduced society's demand for new loans, while giving borrowers incentives to repay the loans more quickly. If the money supply reduced too much, the central bank lowered interest rates, so that the demand for loans increased.

Norway introduced the gold standard in 1873, with a value ratio of 100 NOK for 40 grams of gold. The United States did the same in 1879, with a value ratio of 20.67 USD per ounce of gold. By the turn of the century, virtually the entire world had done the same. Thanks to the gold standard, the money supply remained relatively stable in many places. In some periods, prices also fell.

The introduction of the gold standard worldwide sounds like a positive development. The problem was that suddenly the value of money was no longer *decentralized*. The value of the banknotes did not vary in line with fluctuations in the value of silver or gold, as they did for instance in the Netherlands after the rebellion against the Spanish King. Instead, it was the central banks and the governments that decided the value of the banknotes. Another disadvantage was that it helped coordination of monetary policy at an even greater scale. Eventually, this coordination of the monetary system would also facilitate an even greater degree of inflation – by abandoning the gold standard, keeping the central banking system and beginning to expand the money supply on an international scale.

Before we take a closer look at how the era of the gold standard ended, we can consider that a stable money supply had five important consequences:

(1) the government and the others who had benefited from the inflation tax missed out on a source of revenue
(2) the state became more dependent on collecting ordinary taxes, which was an effective brake on the state's ability to grow or to go to war with other countries
(3) the redistributive effect that inflation had caused ceased, allowing the wealth gap between the richest and everyone else to narrow
(4) there were fewer opportunities to make big money from speculation

(5) whoever wanted to get rich became more dependent on doing honest work and investing their money sensibly

The result must necessarily also lead to increased wealth in society, while at the same time reducing the states' and the financial elites' share. Is this the reason why the gold standard proved to be so short-lived?

**The Federal Reserve – the American central bank system**

According to James Turk, author of *Money and Liberty,* several of the delegates who met in the summer of 1787 to draft the U.S. Constitution believed that inflation was a crime against humanity. However, the battle over what monetary system the newborn nation should have, was something that politicians, not to mention the financial elite, would spend a lot of time and resources on, from the first year of the US Congress well into the 20th century. The US government and its central bank would gradually become the main force in the development of the modern monetary system that we have all over the world today. So, we must take a look at some of the most important developments.

In 1791, Congress passed a law setting up the *First Bank of the United States*. This became the first of several U.S. national banks that were not central banks but were set up to lend money to the federal government.

In 1792, Congress passed *The Coinage Act*. It stated that an employee or official of the mint who fraudulently produces coins of less weight or with less silver or gold than required by law should be punished by death. The law set up a *bi-metallic standard*, while 1 USD was equal to a given weight of gold and a given weight of silver. The ratio of the value of gold and silver was set at 15:1. The government did not issue paper money, and nobody regulated the money supply. Everybody could give silver or gold to the mint and pay a small fee for the minting. The value of the gold and silver dollar varied to some extent with the value of gold and silver, bearing similarities to the system in the Netherlands post-revolution.

A main feature of the US was that they had many independent large and small banks. This system was called "free banking". Some of them succumbed to the temptation to issue more banknotes than they had in *hard money* reserves. The consequence was often the same – a *bank run* and subsequent losses for those holding worthless notes. One striking difference compared with countries who had centralized banking systems was that most of the financial crises that arose were relatively minor and locally delineated.

When the US introduced the gold standard in 1879, they had no central bank or other authorities that had an effective mechanism for enforcing it.

Professor Dr. Murray Rothbard was one of the foremost economists of the Austrian School. Money theory and the history of money were two of his specialties, and he wrote several books on the subject. Rothbard died in 1995. *The Mises Institute* gained access to his manuscripts and used them, among other things, to compile a book entitled *The History of Money and Banking in the United States*, which the institute published in 2002. Rothbard documented that the American financial elite, including banks affiliated with John D. Rockefeller and J.P. Morgan devoted considerable resources to lobbying systematically over a period of many years to set up a central bank in the US.

In 1910, a group of prominent men who were mainly representatives of the American financial elite met. The meeting was held in secret and took place at a luxury resort on Jekyll Island in Georgia. There they drafted the law, which was eventually named *the Federal Reserve Act* and passed by Congress in 1913. The act, which entered into law in 1914, set up a central bank system to set a key interest rate, a.k.a. a key policy rate, as well as the cessation of free banking.

**World War I and the abolition of the gold standard**

When World War I broke out in 1914, customers flocked to the banks and wanted to withdraw their deposits and redeem their banknote holdings in exchange for gold. The banks did not have enough gold in reserve, the officials counting coins as slowly as they could, one-by-one, in the hope that the panic would soon pass. In turn, the European central banks and states reneged on their promises to make up for the banknotes that they had issued in accordance with the amount of gold they had promised their citizens they would receive on demand.

In other words, it took just over 40 years from when many of the countries had established a gold standard that guaranteed that people's money did not fall in value, until they did what Stockholm Banco and Riksens Ständers Bank had done in Sweden. Thus, new national deceptions were a fact. The difference was that this time it spread internationally like falling dominoes. Governments could cover their backs safe in the knowledge that they needed to finance rearmament with loans, with the threat of a major war looming, and that the quickest way to do so was to allow the central bank to expand the money supply. As one can see once again, inflation and war go hand-in-hand.

Suspension of the reclaiming of gold was supposed to be temporary. There is reason to believe that what led to the people allowing the states to do this was that there were a growing number or people worried about threats from abroad. They hoped that their own politicians and central banks would not betray them.

Governments began printing more money, and the money supply increased sharply. This was also the case in Norway, even if we managed to avoid being drawn into the war. By 1918 the M2 money supply had more than tripled. Based on the consumer price statistics, the krone lost about two-thirds of its purchasing power up to 1920. That means the cost of living in Norway tripled in just 6 years. The same thing happened in the UK. Both the Norwegian and British governments borrowed against their means and became heavily laden with debt.

The flood of money encouraged the private banks to increase their lending, which triggered a speculation bubble meaning that very valuable assets ended up in very few hands. When the war ended in 1918, there was an economic crisis not just in in Norway but in most European countries, with poverty and high unemployment running riot. Britain's great era was over, and the state was left with a huge debt to American creditors. The United States, which only joined the war in 1917, was about to take over world financial hegemony. The British pound was losing its status as the world's reserve currency. The age of the dollar was fast-approaching.

**Lenin uses inflation as a weapon**

Following a bloody revolution, the communists took power in Russia in 1917. Dr. Trygve J.B. Hoff is one of the few Norwegians known to belong to the Austrian School. According to his book *Economic Calculation in Socialist Societies*, Lenin was aware that the expansion of the money supply by banks led to a redistribution of society's resources. Hoff writes that "Lenin claimed at the time that money was a capitalist tool for obtaining social goods, for speculating and plundering the workers".

The German philosopher and economist Karl Marx was strongly critical of how the states and capitalists exploited their control over the people through the abuse of the monetary system and was a great inspiration to the communists. Lenin understood that the modern monetary system had been introduced to serve the interests of the financial and political elites, and that it was primarily the common people who lost out. He also knew that the more one increases the money supply, the greater the redistributive effect from the lower classes to the ruling class, led by the financial elites, that class being in league with the Russian Tsarist regime.

Hoff continues:

> By destroying the value of money, it was believed that the remnants of bourgeois society could be eradicated most quickly... From 1 November 1918 to 1 July 1921, the money supply rose to the hundredth, while prices rose to the eightfold.

Lenin expanded the money supply so quickly that those who owned something were unable to exploit any opportunities of the inflation scheme. The state thus kept all the advantages of money printing. The consequence was that bourgeois society and capitalists were stripped, and it became easy for the communists to take over the means of production in society and to get in a position to completely abolish property rights and free markets, in line with the socialist ideals.

The rebels using it as a weapon against their own people in a civil war, the inflation policy proved to be as dangerous a tool as it had been when the monarchs used it in warfare against other countries. By 1921, inflation tipped Russia into a bottomless social crisis with widespread famine and people dying in droves. Thus, the communists had to eat humble pie and reintroduce a kind of market economy, which they called the NEP: the "New Economic Policy". The NEP continued until Stalin introduced a totalitarian planned economy in 1928.

**Hyperinflation in Germany**

When Germany lost World War I in 1918, it had incurred enormous debts. In addition, they had to pay £6.6 billion in reparations.

In retrospect, it is generally agreed that the demands the Germans were subjected to were too great, and that Germany would not be able to get back on its feet economically. The Germans solved this by printing large amounts of money using this to purchase pounds sterling which they then used to pay down their debt. These banknotes were not secured with reserves. This caused what has later been referred to as the hyperinflation in the Weimar republic, which was the informal name of the government of Germany from 1918 to 1933.

In 1944 the great economist of the Austrian school, Ludwig von Mises wrote his book *Omnipotent Government: The Rise of the Total State and Total War.* He explained how he and others had warned the Germans about their monetary policy and that economists, politicians and the media were unable to see the relationship between money printing and price increases:

> The great German inflation was the result of the monetary doctrines of the socialists of the chair... But most of those men who between 1914 and 1923 were in a position to influence Germany's monetary and banking policies and all journalists, writers, and politicians who dealt with these problems labored under the delusion that an increase in the quantity of bank notes does not affect commodity prices and foreign exchange rates. They blamed the blockade or profiteering for the rise of commodity prices, and the unfavorable balance of payments for the rise of foreign exchange rates. They did not lift a finger to stop inflation. Like all pro-inflation parties, they wanted to combat merely the undesirable but inevitable consequences of inflation, i.e., the rise of commodity prices.

Von Mises went on to explain that the Germans' lack of understanding of the problem led them to implement measures that only worsened the situation:

> Their ignorance of economic problems pushed them toward price control and foreign exchange restrictions. They could never understand why these attempts were doomed to fail. The inflation was neither an act of God nor a consequence of the Treaty of Versailles. It was the practical application of the same statist ideas that had begotten nationalism. All the German political parties shared responsibility for the inflation. They all clung to the error that it was not the increase of bank credits but the unfavorable balance of payments that was devaluing the currency.

He also commented on which groups that lost the most, and the political consequences of the hyperinflation:

> The inflation had pauperized the middle classes. The victims joined Hitler. But they did not do so because they had suffered but because they believed that Nazism would relieve them. That a man suffers from bad digestion does not explain why he consults a quack. He consults the quack because he thinks that the man will cure him. If he had other opinions, he would consult a doctor.

The middle class was wiped out. Delusional and desperate Germans flocked to support Hitler.

Money eventually lost all of its value in what was later known as the German hyperinflation. In Berlin, a loaf of bread cost 160 marks at the end of 1922, while a year later it cost 200,000,000,000 marks. In the end, it was impossible to use the money as a means of payment. In the absence of having anything that could function as money, people were driven back to bartering, with the German society being characterized by hunger and poverty. The few who had gold were best equipped to survive in the chaos that ensued. The value of gold did not only increase in value relative to paper money. The scarcity of gold meant that it also gained greater value in relation to other things, such as real estate. On the website *goldsilver.com*, it states that the price of gold rose 1.8 times faster than the general price level.

In 1975 Adam Ferguson wrote his famous book *When Money Dies: The Nightmare of the Weimar Collapse*, where he described how the hyperinflation affected individuals, communities, and institutions, while speculators enjoyed the spoils of political and economic madness:

> There was communal hatred, which was new. There was social resentment, which was new. There was bribery and corruption: that was new. It was the same in Austria and Poland. If you get the same fever, you get the same symptoms...

The corruption among officials in 1924, Lord D'Abernon reported, was 'appalling', whereas before the war bribery had been almost unknown, and a high degree of incorruptibility evident in public and private, if not always in commercial, life... From tax-evasion, food-hoarding, currency speculation, or illegal exchange transactions — all crimes against the State, each of which to a greater or less degree became for individuals a matter of survival — it was a short step to breaching one or other of the Ten Commandments. Whereas the lower classes with the further goad of unemployment might turn to theft and similar crimes (the figures up by almost 50 per cent in 1923 over 1913 and 1925) or to prostitution, the middle and upper classes under a different kind of strain would resort to graft and fraud, bribing, bribable... No people could be expected to remain unconcerned while huge profits and riotous luxury were ostentatiously being enjoyed by the few.

As the old virtues of thrift, honesty and hard work lost their appeal, everybody was out to get rich quickly, especially as speculation in currency or shares could palpably yield far greater rewards than labour... For the less astute, it was incentive enough, and arguably morally defensible, to play the markets and take every advantage of the unworkable fiscal system merely to maintain one's financial and social position.

As that position slid away, patriotism, social obligations and morals slid away with it. The ethic cracked. Willingness to break the rules reflected the common attitude. Not to be able to hold on to what one had, or what one had saved, little as it worried those who had nothing, was a very real basis of the human despair from which jealousy, fear and outrage were not far removed.

The air of corruption in business, politics, and the public service, then, was general. The share capital abuses that became common as more and more shares were concentrated in the hands of profiteers were no more than an example, although a serious one, of the moral deterioration caused by inflation — they largely disappeared when stable money was restored.

**Parity policy and the first gold exchange standard**

The large increase in the money supply after the outbreak of war in 1914 led to a sharp fall in the value of these countries' currencies relative to gold. This meant that those who sold gold demanded more of the countries' currencies in exchange for a given amount of gold than the exchange rate that the states had decided would form the basis for the gold standard.

In 1920, Norges Bank decided to return the Norwegian krone to the value it had measured against gold before the gold redemption obligation was abolished in 1914. This is called "parity policy", where *parity* is the same as *equal*, in the sense of equal value as before. However, it was going to take some time to reach the goal. In 1925, the price of kroner against gold was about twice what it had been below the gold standard. This means that you had to pay about 200 kroner for 40 grams of gold, instead of 100 kroner, as it was with the gold standard. In many other countries, such as France, the value of the currency had fallen even further.

To return the value of the krone to its level as of 1914, Norges Bank had to reduce the money supply. It therefore raised interest rates so that the other banks had to raise their interest rates. In addition, the government regulated banks' lending practices, forcing them to reduce lending. The plan was that people's interest in taking out new loans would fall, and that those who had already taken out loans would be forced to repay the loans more quickly. When the loans were repaid, central banks were able to take that money out of circulation, thereby reducing the money supply. With fewer kroner in circulation, the value of each krone would rise, thusly gold could be bought for fewer kroners.

It was not a significant interest rate increase that was needed. After Norges Bank left the gold standard in 1914, interest rates were around 4%. They then went up to about 6% in 1920, before gradually decreasing towards about 5% in 1928. Importantly, overall monetary policy reduced the money supply, making it expensive for people to raise money to pay instalments. Many were unable to service their loans. It became a landslide of bankruptcy, people went from farm and land, businesses were closed, and unemployment skyrocketed. Private investors, municipalities and the state took over large properties on the cheap. In other words, when Norges Bank achieved its *par* exchange rate target in 1928, monetary policy had done enormous damage, and even today this period is still regarded as the greatest economic crisis we have experienced in modern times in Norway.

It's easier to understand why things went so wrong when you look at the value of what people and businesses borrowed versus the value of what they had to pay back. Parity policy meant that a person who borrowed 100 NOK in 1925 with a repayment agreement in 1928, in reality the customer borrowed 20g of gold and had to repay 40g of gold with the addition of interest. In other words, it would be extremely expensive for the borrower to raise the money in order to service and repay the loan. This broadly explains why the crisis was so widespread.

In Norway, the debate about parity policy has focused on central bank governor Nicolai Rygg's steadfastness and the major political and professional economic discussions that arose in this country. Professor Ragnar Frisch at the University of

Oslo, to whom we will return later in the book, was adamant that the supply of money had to be increased, whilst Rygg was just as adamant that it had to be reduced.

It is less well known that Norway and the other countries that did the same were strongly influenced by a monetary policy game on the behalf of the Bank of England and the Federal Reserve. It was Montagu Norman, governor of the Bank of England, and Benjamin Strong, governor of the central bank in New York, who took the lead. Central to this game was the British goal of re-establishing itself as an economic superpower after going through a very costly First World War. Norman's official position was that the pound sterling had to regain the same high value measured against gold that it had had before the British began printing money during the First World War. At the same time, he wanted to expand the money supply. These two goals would normally not be compatible. If the pound were to increase in value, the British would usually have to reduce, not increase, the money supply. A fundamental prerequisite for Norman to be able to achieve his goals was that the Americans expanded the dollar supply even more than the British expanded the pound. If the Americans didn't, the gold would disappear from Great Britain and end up in the United States. Strong, for his part, also wanted an expansive monetary policy in the US. The two parties therefore had a common interest in trying to achieve this.

In the scheme they developed, the Bank of England was going to fix the value of the pound with respect to a specific weight of gold. No Briton, neither citizen nor business entity, was to be allowed to redeem pounds for gold, with others only entitled to redeem pounds for gold bullion having a minimum weight of 400oz of gold. Walking this path, Norman would make it very difficult for the private sector in Great Britain to demand recompense in gold. The motive was to reduce the chance of a bank run against the Bank of England.

In the book *A history of Money and Banking in the United States*, Rothbard quotes from a letter from Norman to Rygg, in which Norman advised Rygg to introduce the parity policy. Through a combination of persuasion and pressure, Norman managed to convince Norway and all other industrialized countries (except the USA) to introduce the new monetary system. The Scandinavian countries and the Netherlands returned to the same rate of redemption they'd had before the First World War with respect to the value of their currency against gold. Other countries, which had greatly expanded their money supply, could set a new rate against gold which was lower than the redemption rate which they had previously held.

In my opinion, Norman probably understood the following:

- that the national economies of the other countries would enter into a deep recession if they drastically reduced the money supply
- that a growth of the money supply in Great Britain would enable British investors to borrow more money
- British investors would be in a position to make acquisitions for cheap in countries with economic problems

Norman also managed the feat of getting the other countries to hold sterling instead of gold as reserves. If someone demanded redemption of their country's currency, they would therefore receive British pounds instead of gold. And if they had enough pounds, they could demand pounds redeemed in gold bars carrying as they would a minimum of 400oz of gold. In this way, the British had room to maneuver, in that they could expand the money supply without a great risk of the populace running to the bank to demand the redemption of pounds in gold. When the British increased the amount of pounds much of it would end up as reserves in other countries' banks, instead of all the money being used in the UK. The British were thus able to expand the supply of pounds without much risk of the price inflation spiraling out of control in their own country. In this way, the British got into a position to export their monetary inflation to the other countries and increase their money supply to a much greater extent than they could have otherwise done. Newly printed British pounds flowed out of British banks and were used for investment in any country that accepted them as a means of payment. The sellers returned goods, property deeds and securities back to British banks and investors.

The result was an international quasi-gold standard, which has been called the gold exchange standard. It has also been called *the gold bullion standard*.

The disadvantage for the British was that they depended on the American central bank loyally supporting them in expanding the supply of dollar, that the other central banks also had to be loyal to the Bank of England, and that unforeseen events did not happen in the market or in the British economy.

The British began to expand their supply of pounds and the Americans did the same to an even greater extent with their dollars. In short, the British were unable to make the two conflicting desires – to return to a pre-war value of sterling against gold while increasing the money supply – come to pass. Prices and unemployment rose in the UK, industries struggled and the other European central banks, most notably the French, started to voice their discontent with the flood of newly printed pounds.

**The Wall Street crash of 1929**

A significant portion of the newly created money found its way to the stock exchanges. Professor of economics Irving Fisher at Yale University in New Haven, Connecticut was one of those who invested in the stock market. He had grown sizable wealth by inventing a filing system that became standard office equipment all over the United States. In 1929, Fisher was supposedly worth 10 million USD, equivalent to 173 million USD and approximately 1.67 billion NOK in today's money (July 30th, 2022). Fisher went "all in".

The British economist John Maynard Keynes was also comfortable with taking big risks in the stock market. He had lost almost everything he owned in speculation in 1920 but succeeded in rebuilding himself and carried on investing.

The Dow Jones index on the New York Stock Exchange rose from 63 points in 1921 to 381 points in September 1929. The huge rise was due to, among other things, the fact that many people took advantage of the low interest rates to take out loans in order to buy shares. Stories of "ordinary people" getting rich by speculating on stocks spread like wildfire, and millions of people with no experience from finance plunged into speculation. The banks willingly lent against mortgages on people's homes as collateral.

After the stock index peaked, Fisher said that share prices had reached what appeared to be a "permanent high plateau". On 20$^{th}$ September 1929 the inevitable crash became a reality on the London Stock Exchange and on Thursday 24th October the same occurred on the New York Stock Exchange, beginning with a fall of 11%. By November 13th, the paper values of the shares on the New York Stock Exchange had almost halved since their peak. The relationship between monetary inflation and the stock market bubble was well known. Herbert Hoover was president when the crash happened, and he certainly blamed the Federal Reserve. In 1952 he wrote in his memoirs:

> One of these clouds was an American wave of optimism, born of continued progress over the decade, which the Federal Reserve Board transformed into the stock-exchange Mississippi Bubble.

In other words, Hoover drew parallels between what the Federal Reserve did before the crash in 1929 and John Law's scheming in France 200 years earlier.

**The first gold exchange standard is abolished**

The consequences of the crash in 1929 were enormous. There was an unprecedented spate of bankruptcies and unemployment skyrocketed, in the US and in large parts of the Western world, including Norway and Great Britain. The severe depressions led to a cascade of bank runs in 1931, first in Austria, then in Germany, and on September 20th the British threw in the towel and informed that they would not exchange pounds for gold. It was the second time in less than 20 years that the British broke their promise to redeem gold for pounds sterling. This time that decision constituted a breach of contract in relation to the other countries that the British had brought into the agreement on the quasi-gold standard, while at the same time it was an acknowledgment of national bankruptcy. The central banks in France and the Netherlands were left with large holdings of pounds which all at once dropped 30 percent in value relative to gold. What the Bank of England had done to the citizens and businesses of the countries that joined Norman's scheme can best be described as yet another inflation fraud. Despite all of this, he was allowed to continue as governor of the central bank, which would prove to have new, very serious consequences.

Most countries followed Britain's example in abandoning gold and opted for a pure fiat standard. Belgium, the Netherlands, France, Italy and Switzerland decided to stick to the gold standard. Several of the countries entered into currency agreements, where they pegged the rates of their currency against other countries' currencies. Norway and several other countries continued to play the role of monetary vassals to Great Britain, linking their currencies to the British pound with a fixed exchange rate, in what was called a *pound sterling bloc*.

In short, the quasi gold standard that the countries introduced in 1928 was an economic disaster. It was a disaster for Great Britain, which orchestrated it all, for the United States, which played along with Great Britain, and for all the countries that had let themselves be tricked into joining Norman's scheme, including little old Norway.

**President Hoover's 'cure'**

After the crash of the New York Stock Exchange in 1929, US GDP per capita fell by 30% until 1933. Unemployment soared to 25% and the consumer price index fell by almost 25%. The question is if it was market forces or politics that was the cause. In the book *America's Great Depression*, that Murray Rothbard wrote in 1963, he documented in detail that the government intervened in the market on such a scale as it had never done before in the country's history. Rothbard quoted President Hoover's program in his campaign for re-election in the fall of 1932:

> [W]e met the situation with proposals to private business and to Congress of the most gigantic program of economic defense and counterattack ever evolved in the history of the Republic. We put it into action... No government in Washington has hitherto considered that it held so broad a responsibility for leadership in such times... Some of the reactionary economists urged that we should allow the liquidation to take its course until we had found bottom... We determined that we would not follow the advice of the bitter end liquidationists and see the whole body of

> debtors of the United States brought to bankruptcy and the savings of our people brought to destruction.

In short, Hoover would not allow the market to liquidate malinvestments through bankruptcies, something which would have reallocated the assets away from the bankrupt companies and into the hands of more able owners. He tried to repair the damage caused by the Federal Reserve's manipulation of the money supply by manipulating the real economy. And he failed spectacularly.

**President Roosevelt abolishes the gold standard**

Hoover lost the campaign. The winner was Franklin D. Roosevelt, who took office in 1933. After the stock market crash, Keynes had once again lost almost everything he owned. Professor Fisher found himself in an equally difficult situation. He had lost virtually his entire fortune and was forced to sell his house. At the same time, Fisher served as an adviser to Roosevelt. Fisher recommended that the president abandon the gold standard and to begin expanding the money supply. Roosevelt heeded the advice.

To prevent the gold from disappearing out of the country when the United States abolished the gold standard, the authorities prohibited the export of gold. In addition, everyone had to hand over the gold they owned to the US government in return for 20.67 USD per ounce, equivalent to the redemption rate set in 1879. The massive money printing that the central bank had undertaken since that time meant that the compensation received for those who owned gold was hopelessly below market value. This meant that the state effectively confiscated gold. The scheme was straight out of John Law's textbook.

In the book *My father, Irving Fisher (A Reflection book)*, Irving Fisher's son Irving Norton Fisher, presented a letter that the professor wrote to his wife in April 1933. In it, Fisher said that he had saved himself and the family's finances by convincing the President to follow his advice. Rothbard also quoted from the letter in the book *A history of Money and Banking in the United States* with inserted explanations in brackets:

> My next big job is to raise money for ourselves. Probably we'll have to go to Sister [his wife's sister Caroline] again ... I have defaulted payments the last few weekends, because I did not think it was fair to ask Sister for money when there was a real chance that I could never pay it back. I mean that if F.D.R. [Roosevelt] had followed Glass we would have been pretty surely ruined. So would Allied Chemical [in which much of his wife's family fortune was invested], and the U.S. Govt.... Now I can go to Sister with a clean conscience.

The quote shows that Fisher was dependent on convincing Roosevelt to abolish the gold standard, so that the central bank could start expanding the money supply once again. This would lead to the stock market to rise, not to mention the value of Fisher's and his sister-in-law's stocks. The alternative was lasting personal ruin for Fisher and his family. In this case, it is clear that Fisher should not have taken it upon himself to advise the President on which monetary policy would be best for the American people.

When Roosevelt abolished the gold standard, another deception of society came to pass. At the same time, it was in effect an acknowledgment that the US was technically bankrupt.

John F. Wasik, author of the book John Maynard Keynes's Way to Wealth, writes that Keynes was also an adviser to Franklin D. Roosevelt, as well as to UK's finance minister and later Prime Minister Winston Churchill. In a letter to Roosevelt on December 16th, 1933, Keynes offered his compliments to Roosevelt for his decision to abandon the gold standard. In the letter, he also advised that the US government should borrow or print more money as well as increase public spending. Keynes signed the letter thus:

> With great respect,
>
> Your obedient servant J M Keynes

American newspapers printed the letter on December 31st of the same year.

**The outbreak of the World War II and the fight for the gold**

On March 15, 1939, the Germans invaded the Czechoslovakian Republic. The occupiers coerced central bank employees to telegraph a message to the Bank of England to transfer the Czechoslovakians' gold holdings from the Czechoslovakians' reserve account to the Germans' reserve account. Governor Montagu Norman, knowing full well that the Czechoslovakians Republic had been invaded, executed the order. In this way, Germany managed to sell 50 tons of gold that belonged to the Czechoslovakians Republic. Norman's role in the German seizure of the Czechoslovakians gold was a scandal that ostensibly contributed greatly to the British Government nationalizing the Bank of England in 1946. However, inexplicably, the scandal was kept a secret from the public until 2013.

On 1 September 1939, Germany attacked Poland. Polish authorities withdrew holdings of 79.5 tons of gold from their central bank and after a long journey the gold wended its way to New York.

Towards the end of 1940, Belgium moved 200 tons of its gold reserves to England, 200 tons to the United States and Canada, and 200 tons to France. The Belgian gold that the French had their hands on found its way to Berlin, after the Vichy government made an agreement with Germany to release French prisoners of war. France managed to save its own gold reserves.

The Norwegian authorities did not decide to move their gold until the day of invasion, April 9th, 1940. Norwegian civilians and elite soldiers barely managed to get approx. 50 tons of gold out, which ended up in England. This story is yet another example of how naive Norwegian authorities could be. They should have secured the gold at a much earlier stage. However, we will soon see yet another example that the Norwegian authorities are not alone in their naivete with respect to monetary policy.

**The Bretton Woods agreement of 1944**

As World War II drew to a close, the United States, the Soviet Union, Great Britain, Norway and 40 other countries met at the Mount Washington Hotel in Bretton Woods, New Hampshire in the United States. The States finally agreed that one ounce of gold, 31.1 grams, should be priced at 35 dollars, and that the other countries should tie their currency to the dollar: that is to say, they decided upon a fixed exchange rate. The agreement, which was called the "Bretton Woods Agreement", was to become a new gold exchange standard.

This time only the central banks and the states were to have the right to demand that dollars be redeemed for gold. No one else, neither companies nor private individuals, should have a legal claim to do this. The motive was of a kind with the first gold exchange standard – to reduce the risk of a bank run. The United States was to keep its reserves in gold, while the other countries were to keep their reserves in dollars. The parties ratified the agreement in 1946. The Soviet Union chose to stay out of it, because they believed that it was the American financial elite who were behind this scheme. Sweden and West Germany joined the agreement in 1951 and 1952 respectively.

In practice this meant that the parties introduced something very nearly a global currency. The core of the agreement was similar to the gold exchange standard that ended in 1931, only now the Americans were in the driver's seat at the expense of the British. The Americans began to expand the dollar supply. This gave the other central banks increased access to dollars and thus they could also increase their dollar reserves, which gave them the opportunity to expand their own currencies. In other words, the scheme meant that the other countries expanded their money on the basis of reserves consisting of dollars, while the Americans expanded their dollars on the basis of an ever smaller, in a relative sense, gold reserve.

As the value of the other countries' money was pegged to the dollar, it was the United States that received the greatest benefits. In practice, the scheme meant that the dollar became "bankable currency" globally. The US could thus "export" its inflation in exchange for goods from all over the world, while there was less risk of prices running wild domestically.

In 1945, Roosevelt and the Saudi Arabian head of state King Abdul Aziz Ibn Saud met to discuss a strategic cooperation for the post-war era. This resulted in a bi-lateral agreement in 1951 which, among other things, meant that the US would give Saudi Arabia military protection on the proviso that Saudi Arabia sell its oil for a dollar price. Saudi Arabia was such a large oil producer that it led to a dollar price across the entire oil market. As oil grew to become the largest and most valuable of all commodities, it led to a huge demand for dollars. Dollar-based international oil trade thus functioned as a buffer against price inflation in the US.

Together, the Bretton Woods agreement and the dominance of the dollar in the oil market gave the Americans enormous room for maneuver in monetary policy, which they also knew how to exploit. The US could run large deficits financed by government loans. Those who gave loans to the United States saw it as a safe bet, because they knew that the Federal Reserve was a willing buyer of the government debt in the secondary market. When the US central bank bought the US government bonds, it did so by printing money which then flooded the world markets. For the Americans, this scheme functioned as a straw into the financial resources everywhere where the dollar was accepted, that is to say, all over the world.

Just like Harald Hardråde and Charles XII, the Americans used their position to strengthen their armed forces. One can imagine that the flow of newly printed dollars went on a journey from the US and that those who received them sent metals and other real resources back, which the Americans used to make, for example, tanks, ships, planes, uniforms, firearms, ammunition and everything else that they needed. The inflation policy also helped the Americans finance their conflicts in Korea and Vietnam.

**The Nixon shock**

As the money supply increased, matters proceeded as would be expected with these sorts of schemes. To an even greater extent than previous iterations, it was now the central banks who lined up in what was to become an international bank run against the Federal Reserve. Confidence in money plummeted, central banks exchanged more and more dollars for gold, which in turn reduced Americans' gold reserves. Pressure on the Federal Reserve increased. Soon it would be unable to make good on its promise to redeem dollars for gold at the fixed rate.

In 1971, President Richard Nixon made history, the networks willing participants, when they broadcasted his message that the Americans would not keep their promise. The US lifted the bond with effect from March 1973. Nixon packaged his message as if this was good news and indeed sensible policy. As was the case when the British abolished the earlier quasi-gold standard, the American decision was in effect a breach of contract and an admission of bankruptcy all at once. The British and the Americans also now held in common that they had reneged on their promise to exchange currency for gold *twice*, the British in 1914 and 1931, the Americans in 1933 and 1971.

It hardly came as a great surprise to the other countries' central banks, which had probably been aware all along that the quasi gold standard was a thinly veiled pyramid scheme within which everyone was given the opportunity to expand their currency. Many of them also had experience of a completely parallel event, when the Bank of England broke its promise to redeem sterling against gold in 1931, thirteen years before they entered into the Bretton Woods agreement.

How much the politicians had understood of this when the countries entered into the new agreement in 1944 is open to debate. After Nixon's TV appearance, the populace probably began to wonder who really controlled the central banks, whether it was the governments, the Federal Reserve, or the financial elites. In any case, it is a fact that Nixon's message came as a shock to an international community that no longer knew anything about the history of monetary policy. What the kings had previously done to their people, on a largely national basis, the Americans had now done on an almost global scale. The United States had pursued a monetary policy that undoubtedly constituted the biggest fraud in world history up to that time.

The US Federal Reserve's St. Louis branch publishes an overview of the *money supply M2* going back to January 1959. Up to March 1973, according to this statistic, the dollar supply increased by 284%, that is, almost tripling in just 14 years. This corresponds to an average increase per year of approximately 8%.

**Stagflation in the 1970s**

After Nixon revealed that the United States would not exchange dollars for gold, the demand for gold rose. In 1973, the official price went up from 35 USD to 125 USD per ounce, which translates to a devaluation of the dollar of 72%. In the 1970's, many of the Western countries experienced economic decline, with a combination of high inflation and high unemployment, something economists called stagflation. However, the hegemony of the dollar was not over. Many creditors had no interest in the dollar collapsing completely. The US was also still a military superpower. Nearly all of the countries switched to a pure fiat money policy, where the dollar continued to function as the banks' reserve currency.

**Petrodollar**

When the Americans left the second quasi gold standard, they risked the dollar losing its dominance as the world's reserve currency. The solution was oil: In 1973, Nixon and Secretary of State Henry Kissinger entered into an agreement with Saudi Arabia that the US would sell weapons to Saudi Arabia in exchange for Saudi Arabia continuing to sell oil for dollars. Alternatively, Saudi Arabia could buy American government bonds, which is to say, give loans to the American authorities for the oil revenues. This was a further development of the agreement that the countries entered into in 1951. By 1975, all OPEC countries began selling oil for dollars.

This had, among other things, six important consequences:

(1) Purchases and sales in the global energy and commodity markets were transacted in dollars
(2) Anyone who would buy these goods had to obtain dollars
(3) The US could supply the world with all the dollars it needed by expanding its money supply
(4) The US federal government could take out huge loans at a low cost
(5) The US federal government could use the world's demand for dollars to finance large budget deficits, and continually refinance its debt obligations by taking out new loans
(6) The US federal government could expand the government through debt-financed budget deficits

In this way, the Americans could continue to boast that they held the world's reserve currency: these days, the common sobriquet is *petrodollar*.

**Arms race and continued dollar dominance**

American military power was seen by many countries as a guarantor that the Soviet Union would not expand its territories further. This helped to enable the US to continue its inflation policy. If the Soviet Union had not had ambitions to seed its political system to ever-larger parts of the world, it is unlikely that so many countries would have agreed to continue as subjects of the United States' monetary policy in a dollar-dominated world.

The communists' policy, which was based on a socialist planned economy, did not produce the same redistributive effect that the Americans received with their inflation policy, and with which they could use to arm themselves. The communists relied to a much greater extent on coercion, rather than forcing people to "voluntarily" send their resources to them from far and wide in exchange for rubles. Coercion is costly, and centralized planning of an economy does not work well. The Soviet Union therefore only dug ever downwards into its own economic misery. As a result of this, and many more things besides, the superpower imploded in a spectacular fashion in 1991. Hyperinflation, with up to 200 percent general price increases, created economic chaos which invariably helped a small number of oligarchs to rise from the Soviet Union's ashes to become an important part of Russia's new political elite.

**'Climate currency'**

When the US Congress passed *The Clean Air Act* in 1990, it introduced a market for trading in so-called *climate credits*. A climate credit is a politically created security, which has its roots in rules on the regulation of industrial emissions of greenhouse gases. The US also ensured that the UN decided in 1997 that the countries should facilitate a global market for climate quotas.

By the end of 2021, the total market for climate allowances had a value of approximately 850 billion USD, i.e., 0.85 trillion USD. This is, for example, approximately one trillion less than one year's total income globally as a result of the extraction of oil and natural gas. The market is growing rapidly, and many economists have advocated that climate quotas could form the basis for a new global currency. Most of the trading of climate credits are traded in dollars. This market is, therefore, much like the oil market, a channel that functions as a form of buffer against general price inflation in the US and which enables the Federal Reserve to continue the expansion of the money supply.

**Euro**

In 1998, twelve EU countries introduced a monetary union with the euro as the common currency and a common central bank headquartered in Frankfurt, Germany. The common European market made the euro rise as the second largest currency worldwide. New EU member states, which traditionally had weak economies, were not allowed to join, while Sweden, Denmark and Great Britain chose to abstain from membership.

Norway, which is not an EU member, derives the majority of its income from taxation of the sales of oil and gas priced in dollars, continued with a purely fiat standard. Switzerland, continued with a gold standard until 2000.

**Cryptocurrency**

The gradual transition from coins and notes to debit and credit cards eventually led to fiat money presenting as an electronic currency. The next great innovation in money arose outside the sphere of governments. In recent years, a number of private means of payment have appeared, which are so-called *cryptocurrencies*.

Bitcoin was the progenitor. It is also the most popular cryptocurrency, as it is not based on any kind of reserve. It therefore also has similarities with fiat money. No one knows who invented Bitcoin. One *Satoshi Nakamoto*, the name most certainly being a pseudonym, posited and distributed the idea during the financial crisis in

2008 and it was put into practice in 2009. The creators encoded the text, "The Times 03/Jan/2009 Chancellor on brink of second bailout for banks", into the first Bitcoin bloc that was created. Many have interpreted the text as if Bitcoin is a protest against the state-controlled monetary system with its creators as opponents of fiat money.

Bitcoin is based on so-called *blockchain technology*. Payment is made directly between buyer and seller without the need to use banks as intermediaries. The money is "mined" by computers which are left with nebulous calculations. Everyone can take part in the mining. This money system is thus completely decentralized, a feature that it shares with monetary systems based on metal coins. Bitcoin differs from the currency of governments in that it is programmed that the growth in the supply of Bitcoins falls towards zero. The program is designed in such a way that there can only be a maximum of 21 million Bitcoins 'in circulation'. The designers have therefore planned for Bitcoin to grow more valuable over time, which would mean it will have a deflationary effect. With the exception of market fluctuations as a result of continuous changes in supply and demand in the "secondary market", this becomes a reality.

The mining of Bitcoin is power-intensive, and there are many people and companies who have invested large sums of money in the mining and purchase of this cryptocurrency. One of the reasons why it requires so much electricity, is because it enables the miners' computers to provide the network with a constant high level of security. This is necessary to safeguard against hacking and other types of cybercrimes.

Demand has risen sharply. From September 11th, 2020, to November 12, 2021, the price rose from 94,000 NOK to 560,000 NOK per Bitcoin, i.e., by almost 600%. Afterwards, the prices have more than halved, and at the time of writing (August 17th, 2022) the price is 230,000 NOK.

Some people say that Bitcoin is a "hard currency" because, like gold and silver, its quantity is limited. Many claim that most other cryptocurrencies have more in common with fiat money than Bitcoin, and refer to the fact they are centralized, do not require time and energy for "mining" and that they can be expanded indefinitely in principle.

Proponents of Bitcoin also point out that the Bitcoin technology facilitates virtually cost-free direct payment between buyer and seller. This infrastructure gradually competes with the banks' own infrastructure for interbank settlements.

The states have so far chosen not to protect their money monopoly against this development. A first impulse would be to think that it is strange that the states have not banned this upstart competitor. There may be several reasons why they have not done so, which we will return to later.

According to US media outlet CNBC, in 2022 there will be more than 19,000 different cryptocurrencies. Time magazine reported in November 2021 that the cryptocurrency market was worth approximately 3 trillion USD, equivalent to one-tenth of the United States' gross domestic product (GDP). By the summer of 2022, the total value of the world's cryptocurrency had fallen to approximately 1 trillion USD. This means that the cryptocurrency market was then slightly more valuable than the market for climate quotas.

Another innovation are virtual worlds where "citizens" can buy real estate, clothes and food with cryptocurrencies that is referred to as *non-fungible tokens* (NFT's). CNBC reported on January 12, 2022, that someone had paid 450,000 USD to become rap artist Snoop Dogg's neighbor in a virtual world called Sandbox. In other words, a speculative market for cryptocurrency has arisen, which in turn can be used for speculation in virtual worlds.

The development propagates quickly, and governments try to figure out how the various types of cryptocurrencies should be regulated. For instance, if a certain cryptocurrency should be defined and regulated as commodities or as securities.

# The economists

**Introduction**

As mentioned, it is now approximately 100 years since the great discussion between the economists about inflation was settled, in that it was those who were in favor of inflation who won in the eyes of the politicians. In this chapter, we explore some developments in economics from the 19th century up to the present day. The reasons for that big discussion regarding inflation among economists in the 20th century lies partly in the development of the method used and partly in how the research was financed. We will also look at how economists influenced politicians and therefore economic policy.

The aim of the chapter is primarily to shed light on the reasons why the economists from the Austrian school fought so fiercely against the inflation policy. Before we go any further, we can summarize some of the main underlying reasons why many economists began to think that inflation was a good thing:

- A political shift in the direction of a more positive view of the government's role, both in general and as a socio-economic actor
- Strong incentives, in that the financial elite funded researchers who supported inflation
- Economic history lost recognition as a subject, it was considered anecdotal knowledge, and it was claimed that it could not provide a basis for true inferences
- Deductive method gradually lost recognition as a method in economics
- The natural sciences, with statistics, empiricism and mathematics, were eventually considered the only thing that could form a scientific basis for socio-economic analysis
- A lack of skepticism towards the Soviet Union's reporting of economic progress

I have chosen to highlight classical economics, Keynesianism, the Oslo School, the Austrian School and monetarism, as it is in these schools of thought within economics that are most often referred to in discussions about inflation.

**Classical economics**

The field of economics emerged in the 18th and 19th centuries, growing in parallel to the industrial revolution. It was characterized by the use of deduction, a method in which logic is applied based on basic laws and principles. A common example of deduction is that "all birds have feathers", and that "all sparrows are birds", and therefore "all sparrows have feathers".

Using logical principles, the economists derived logical consequences, for example how the price of an item developed as a result of supply and demand in a marketplace. The starting point for the use of the deductive method in economics was natural law's recognition of man's right to own himself, the right to own things (property rights), the right to trade with others, people's desire to improve their situation and so on. The economists derived conclusions on the basis of knowledge about man and interaction between people in a society with scarce resources. Richard Cantillon, Anne Robert Jacques Turgot, Jean Baptiste Say, Claude-Frederic Bastiat, David Richardo, and Adam Smith are examples of well-known economists who are linked to the classical school.

When the Austrian Carl Menger, as one of three contemporary economists, deduced in the 1870's that 'man acts on the basis of a principle of subjective marginal utility', it was an important step forward for the school of economics. We can take an example based on the valuation of something that has a positive marginal utility: The first jacket you own has the most value to you, the next marginally a little less, etc. The more jackets you have, the less value each new jacket holds for you. This means that the more jackets you have, the more you will be willing to give one of them away, rather than to keep it. Conversely, you may have negative marginal benefit, for example if you have eaten a lot of cake, eating another piece may make you feel unwell, another piece causes stomachache and so on down the line until there is either no cake left, or you've collapsed into a gluttonous heap on the floor.

Menger emphasized that man's appreciation of economic goods is subjective. This means that you cannot compare two people's "scale" for valuing goods or their inherent value. Andrea, for example, makes sure to have enough wood for two winters, while Barry, for his part, thinks it's enough to have wood for one winter at a time. In the same way, Barry prioritizes gathering so many berries that he has enough for the next two years, while Andrea thinks it's enough to have berries for one year at a time. They assess value completely differently, because they have different preferences, therein lying the essence of the human condition. Our valuation of economic goods, whether in relation to consumption, savings or investment, is subjective.

Based on a number of such definitions and findings, the economists were able to analyze complex relationships that helped to explain society and the economy. They could also use these tools to analyze how different types of governmental interventions would affect society. For example, how would imposing a tax on sugar affect the buying and selling of sugar? And how, for example, would introducing market privileges such as monopolies affect prices and output?

The analyses of the economists in the classical tradition showed that interference from the state would mean that the market players would be less able to meet people's needs. Most of them therefore believed that the state should limit itself to protecting the people from war and crime, as well as protecting property rights and ensuring that agreements were respected. It is common to refer to this as a *laissez faire* economy, which is to say, where the government does not interfere with the business of private actors.

**New methods and the Rockefeller Foundation**

Towards the end of the 19th century, economists began to experiment more with the use of empirical methods, inspired as they were by the natural sciences. The economists then typically focused on the national state-of-things, state institutions, the states' statistics on the country's production, consumption, employment, exports, imports and money supply, etc. They increasingly turned their focus towards what was best for society and for the state, as well as which institutional conditions could best ensure that society's resources were used in the most efficient way possible. This was a paradigm shift, where the state, on one hand, became an important independent actor in economics, both as owner, producer, consumer and regulator, while the economist, on the other hand, became an adviser who could guide the state so that society's use of resources could be optimized.

If we compare this with the values that were the basis of the classical tradition's tools for analyzing the economy, we see that the change meant that the state began to constitute a significant intrinsic value. The observant reader will understand what contradictions then arose, as the state's growth necessarily presupposed active interventions in property rights, which were the very foundation of the analytical tools in the classical tradition.

This development also paved the way for analyses of and experimentation with the state, as well as the economist as a social planner who directs the economy and manages economic development. The Rockefeller Foundation used large resources to finance research in economics. The foundation's money came from John D. Rockefeller, who was the founder of the Standard Oil Company. Rockefeller became the world's richest man, and eventually he and his family became a significant player in the financial markets and banking. As previously mentioned, Rockefeller was also one of those people who had bankers in his employ that lobbied hard for the United States to have its own central bank.

Beardsley Ruml, who had a social science background and a doctorate in psychology, designed the foundation's guidelines for what the money should be used for in 1923. He wrote:

> *[P]roduction from the universities is largely deductive and speculative, on the basis of second-hand observations, documentary evidence and anecdotal material. It is a small wonder that the social engineer finds this social science abstract and remote, of little help to him in the solution of his problems.*

Ruml considered that the subject of economics was unscientific and an obstacle to social progress. The statement was an attack on the classical economics, where Ruml slandered the economists' methods by putting the word *speculative* as close to the word *deductive* as possible. For academics and universities around the world, such statements sent a clear signal about what the foundation would spend money on, and which academic priorities could become an argument for the foundation to withdraw its financial support.

However, the answers that the methods and analyses within the classical tradition of economics gave did not suggest that it would be right to put someone in charge of "social engineering", i.e., someone who would build and manage society, through centralized government planning, as Ruml postulated was necessary. The understanding that the economists in the classical tradition had developed was that introducing a kind of quasi-engineering or quasi-scientific method within the field of economics would fail. The answers that classical economics gave to such questions were that the economy in society is too complex and, in total, the result of millions of people's individual and ever-changing needs, preferences and choices. The analyses carried out by the economists within the classical tradition also showed that attempts to engage in economic social planning with state interventions in trade and property rights would damage economic development.

However, Rockefeller's priorities were good news for many progressive academics around university campuses in the United States and Europe. In 2007, David Lee Seim wrote an article as part of his doctoral thesis in the history of technology and science, a thesis he named: *Perhaps we can hit upon some medium of course: Rockefeller philanthropy, economic research, and the structure of social science – 1911-1946.*

Seim refers to, among other things, that economists at the University of Stockholm approached Ruml in 1924 in order to obtain support for economic research. They argued that Sweden was in many ways an almost "ideal laboratory", and pointed out that the country was small, governed in an orderly manner and had a homogeneous population. This made it easier to collect the necessary statistical and material basis, as well as to isolate and study social phenomena. The argument reflected the shift that was taking place in the field of economics, moving it as it did in the direction of becoming a subject where repeated numerical experiments were carried out as a basis for recommendations about which planned economic policy was best for the state.

The problem was that in real life, assumptions change continuously, in contrast to the mathematical models that the progressive economists developed. The economy is dynamic, develops through entrepreneurship and innovation, and is inhibited by sudden crises related to, for example, war, extreme weather events, climate change, natural disasters and disease – 'force majeure' events. The frameworks conditions and dynamics change continuously, and none of the market participants, neither producers, sellers, buyers nor intermediaries, has a crystal ball. Society at large cannot, therefore, be placed in a laboratory. It is not possible to control or conduct experiments with society's economy without introducing totalitarian systems or manipulating the results in some way.

It makes sense then to know that the economists were influenced by the rise of a socialist centrally planned economy in the Soviet Union. The levers of the state in the Kremlin notoriously misreported and exaggerated its figures on economic growth, and both professionals and politicians were fooled for decades. Running in parallel to this, the West struggled with crisis after crisis in the 1920s and 1930's. Many blamed free markets and capitalism, at the time unable as they were to understand that it was the governments' and central banks' manipulation of the money supply in society that was responsible for the major economic fluctuations. The rise of fascism and socialism posed a constant threat to the security of western countries. Seim highlights how such conditions affected Ruml and other important internal and external contributors to the foundation.

Statistics Norway's article, *The Norwegian post-war economy,* written in 1965, adequately illustrates the problems that economist using the new methods would have to struggle with:

> But the hypothesis of proportionality between real capital and production is impossible to reconcile with some of the empirical material available. Thus, the post-war observations of the connection between investment level and growth, compare diagram 8 above, directly contradict this hypothesis. Doubt is also created by the results of empirical studies from many countries of growth since the turn of the century and earlier. These investigations clearly point in the direction that far from the entire increase in production over a longer period of time can be explained by a greater investment of work and capital under constant technique; they therefore show that productivity progress — whatever it may be due to — must have been an important factor behind the growth.

> Under the impression of such empirical results, theoretical research has oriented itself away from models that assume "constant technique". They can hardly be realistic, since they ignore something that, by all accounts, is absolutely essential to the growth process.

The level of employment and invested capital could therefore not explain the economic growth. The problem for the economists lay in their failure to calculate what innovation and other productivity improvements contributed. This led to the inclusion of innovation and knowledge development as variable factors in their mathematical models. The economic growth that could not be explained by employment and invested capital had to be explained by a productivity improvement factor '*X*' that changed in an unpredictable way.

**Keynesianism**

John Maynard Keynes became the most influential economist in the world from ca. 1920, an influence that sustained throughout most of the 20th century. In contrast to most economists in the classical tradition, he believed that the state should play an active role in the economy and that it should expand the money supply when necessary. Additionally, he suggested they pursue an active fiscal policy, by saving tax revenues when the economy was buoyant and by using money on public projects when growth showed signs of slowing. Keynes believed that the combination of an active fiscal policy and a flexible monetary policy would ensure full employment and full use of capital. A consequence of the theory was also that a sufficiently large increase in the money supply ruled out the possibility of high unemployment.

Keynes' theories of managing society's economy are akin to how a factory owner might retool machines, production lines and overall productivity, etc., so that the factory becomes as profitable as possible. He advocated a market economy with a strong element of centralized planning by state means. Keynes placed great emphasis on mathematics and the empirical method with, among other things, extensive use of statistics on production and unemployment. That is to say, social economics was something that had to be studied with a basis on all numbers in society that were relevant to the economy and its development. This way of doing things bears similarities to those experiments undertaken in the natural sciences, for example physics. Society, with its production, consumption, employment, real estate, energy and other capital, was Keynes' 'laboratory'.

Keynes was opposed to the gold standard, and emphasized, among other things, that it was problematic in salary negotiations that the value of money can increase over time (deflation) when it is anchored in gold. He pointed out that the workers' organizations found it difficult to accept wage cuts even though they were sometimes necessary in connection with adjustment phases and pointed out that deflation would make this even more challenging. In contrast, inflation could mask a fall in real wages that was not so easy for the workers' unions to spot. If workers did not understand that inflation was eating into their wages, it would be easier for employers to get them to accept offers that in reality effectively were, after inflation adjustment, pay cuts.

Helped by Professor Irving Fisher's corresponding theories and methods, Keynes's views gained influence in American practical politics after the stock market crash of 1929 onwards towards the Second World War. In the 1930s, the American state implemented, among other things, huge public development projects, employment of 8.5 million people in the public sector and financial support for the agricultural industry. President Roosevelt called the program "The New Deal". The policy spread to many other countries around the world, thus welfare states were born.

If you want to understand why Keynes was so popular with politicians, it is useful to consider that Keynes' theory assumed that politicians and civil servants had to play an absolutely central role in the economy. For those who wanted a bigger state, more taxation, more regulation, and more centralized planning, boasting the support of Keynes, Fisher et al was an invaluable gift. This must also be viewed through the prism that economists of the classical tradition were essentially opposed to such a development. Economists therefore evolved from them acting as the yoke on the state's growth to becoming the principal accelerator of it.

John F. Wasik writes in his book about Keynes that he was a skilled stock speculator, but also that he was a risk-taker. In addition to losing almost everything he owned in both 1920 and 1929, the same thing happened again in 1937. Afterwards, Keynes still managed to accumulate a considerable fortune.

The similarity between John Law, Irving Fisher and John Maynard Keynes is striking. All three were speculators and advisers to heads of state and lost their fortunes in one way or another in the financial market. All despised gold, all "loved" fiat money, and all believed that putting more money into circulation would solve problems when the economy would not move in the right direction.

Fisher and Keynes also had in common that the stock market crash of 1929 robbed them of their fortunes. Both were also advisors to President Roosevelt, who we saw followed Fisher's advice, and who went on to repeal the gold standard, confiscate privately owned gold, expand the money supply, and using borrowed money and taxpayers' money on a slew of public projects to "save the economy" in the United States. Coincidentally, this policy also became the salvation of Fisher's personal finances. The extent to which Keynes helped himself to the fruits of the economy whilst at the same time offering advice to the heads of state is unclear, but he was most assuredly in a significantly better position to do so than the ordinary private investor.

Keynes left a deep, indelible mark on the design of economic policy in large parts of the world. He became a very important factor for the development of the subject of economics, including in American academia. After the Second World War, a professor colleague of Fisher's at Yale University, James Tobin became known as one of the foremost Keynesians in the United States.

**The American financial elite and the Oslo School**

Murray Rothbard has written extensively about how the American financial elite and representatives of the federal government worked to get both the United States and other countries to implement a monetary policy that served their interests. His presentation in the book *The History of Money and Banking in the United States* provides a good picture of the dynamics of what is called "rent seeking activity". This is a term used to describe special interests' work to influence the authorities to yield advantages at the expense of everyone else. The book shows that the Americans worked systematically in country after country to put in place a monetary policy that suited the American government and the financial elite.

The story of how Americans influenced the development of Norwegian economic policy illustrates how simple these mechanisms can be. In his article Seim highlights that the Rockefeller Foundation's work was about finding young academic talents, inviting them to the USA on research grants, and letting some of them build completely new research institutes in their home country based on the new and "scientific" use of methods.

In 1926, Ragnar Frisch finished his doctorate in theoretical statistics at the University of Oslo. The Rockefeller Foundation awarded Frisch a scholarship and he was subsequently granted a VISA in order to stay in the USA from 1927-1928. This was the start of a long-lasting collaboration between Frisch and the foundation. He used the foundation's headquarters in New York as his base. There he formed lasting ties with several prominent American economists, including Professor Irving Fisher. Together they founded The Econometric Society in 1930. Fisher invited him to Yale University where he received a residency during the years 1930-1931. Frisch also received an offer to become a professor at Yale, with an annual salary of 7,000 USD, equivalent to approximately 130,000 USD, in today's money. Fisher was to pay part of his salary, as a donation to the university.

The Rockefeller Foundation offered to finance the establishment of a research institute at the University of Oslo, on condition that Frisch was appointed as head of the institute. Instead of becoming a professor at Yale, Frisch chose to accept the offer from the foundation. He was also appointed directly by the Storting (the Norwegian parliament) as a professor, which was very unusual. According to a "Memorandum" on Frisch from 2018 written by Olav Bjerkholt at the Department of Economics at the University of Oslo, the Rockefeller foundation financed dozens of employees who became the basis for Frisch's scientific life.

According to Seim, in the years 1931 – 1937 the foundation supported the economics institutes at the universities of Berlin, Bonn, Budapest, Krakow, Leuwen, Paris, Sofia, Stockholm, Vienna, Oslo, Kiel, Heidelberg, Rotterdam and Bucharest, of which the last five received the most money.

Soon after Frisch took up the position of professor and head of department in 1932, he began to get involved in more than just research and teaching. On his own initiative he secured a meeting with the Prime Minister, prominent parliamentarians and leaders in the banking and business sectors. At the meeting, he handed out a memorandum in which he presented his assessment of how the state could solve the economic crisis that Norway was mired in. He argued that when financial resources in the real economy were not fully used, such as labor and capital, it was due to consumers not having enough money. One of the solutions was to stimulate credit growth.

In 2014, the historian, now associate professor at the USN Business School Eivind Thomassen, wrote the article *Financial power – people power, the Labor Party and the demand for democratization of Norges Bank approx. 1920–49*, in which the following illustrative paragraphs appear:

> Ragnar Frisch tried in the early 1930's, through newspaper articles, notes and meetings, to get the majority in the Storting to change the framework for monetary policy, or to get Norges Bank to pursue a more expansive monetary policy...
>
> Frisch's (and other progressive economists') assessment of monetary policy in the 1920's and early 1930's became a very strong inspiration for many of the economists who took leading positions under the post-war Labor Party government. Not least, many of these, trained under Frisch, were given central positions in the powerful Ministry of Finance. Here, important management functions for the economic policy came to be centralized, at the expense of, among others, Norges Bank.
>
> For economic analysis, "mutual claims between the state and Norges Bank had as little interest as claims between husband and wife for the finances of a private household", claimed two of the post-war leading social economists in 1945.

In other words, it took a short amount of time since Frisch started in his new position until he began to take several initiatives imploring Norwegian politicians to support an increase in the money supply. The economists, whom he educated, were also greatly influenced by his theories, and the last sentence quoted above clearly shows that economic history cannot have been given high priority in the teaching.

Frisch quickly became a dominant personality in academic circles, and disagreements arose with economists who were not supporters of his views on the subject as well as the development of the program of study. Frisch was not careful with the way in which he presented himself, believing that economics needed to be taken "out of the fog", and furthermore claimed that his opponents belonged to what he called "the unenlightened plutocracy". Professor Ingvar Wedervang, one of his colleagues, was one of his opponents, and when Wedervang accepted the offer to become headmaster of the business school in Bergen, Frisch was left as the winner of the hegemony within the economics department at the University of Oslo. According to the article Ragnar Frisch and the *Postwar Norwegian Economy by Arild Sæther* and Ib E. Eriksen, he established himself as a "house master" at the Department of Economics.

During the latter half of the 1930's, Frisch became increasingly skeptical of free markets, and an increasingly strong supporter of a planned economy. Investors and entrepreneurs had no place in the economy, and it was the social economists who should make the important investment decisions.

Frisch became the founder of the so-called *Oslo School*, which posited that quantitative methods based on mathematics and statistics were the only thing that could be considered scientific within the subject of economics. He proved to be a true radical in the economic sense, when he rejected the idea that interest is the price of capital. This is a little like saying an apple tumbling to the ground has nothing to do with gravity. In short, Frisch contributed greatly to turning the subject of economics completely on its head. Economists educated in Norway before and after Frisch rose to prominence probably only had the title, and little else in common. Sæther and Eriksen write:

> Through his strong, domineering personality and his habit of disseminating by privileged mimeos his own ideas and judgments, Frisch provided graduates of the Oslo School with an exceptional confidence in the science of economics. Jens Christopher Andvig (1993, 29) writes: "Their confidence was easy to understand because they knew about the complex, but simple world of the 'real' economy. It was knowledge which was exclusive to them and it had been introduced to them by an intellectual genius.

The Oslo School also became part of what was called *The Iron Triangle*, a term used by journalists and academics in the social sciences community to describe the close ties between the three institutions: the Department of Economics at the University of Oslo; Statistics Norway; and the Ministry of Finance. These were the same state institutions which in the post-war period contributed the most to shaping economic policy in Norway. In practice, for a long time it was about continuing much of the planned economy when Norway was an occupied territory, including rationing, price regulation and regulation of the use of real estate. The Oslo School promoted a high degree of public investment. It was also economists from the Oslo School who prepared the macroeconomic models that Norges Bank uses in implementing its monetary policy today.

Like many of his contemporaries, Frisch spoke warmly of the economic system of the Soviet Union. He was beguiled by the fantastical figures that the regime in the Kremlin pumped out by way of its propaganda apparatus, and in a letter to Trygve J.B. Hoff in 1958 he praised the communists for having an economy without a harmful business cycle while at the same time having 7 to 8 percent annual economic growth. In a later letter, he corrected this to 10 percent. Sæther and Eriksen explain:

> Frisch and his supporters rejected the ability of a free enterprise economy to allocate resources effectively. Frisch compared an economist to a social engineer who has a toolkit consisting of new mathematical planning models, a system of detailed national accounts and detailed regulations and controls. With this toolkit he could beneficially govern the economy. An economist with the right training could assist the politicians in government and parliament to develop the welfare state. Until his death Frisch defended what he called rational economic planning and claimed that it was superior to a market economy.

Here we see the term "social engineer" being used in full accordance with Beardsley Ruml's vision in the Rockefeller Foundation's guidelines for the allocation of funds.

Frisch's dominant position in the development of economics and economic policy meant that Norway would become one of the countries that would have a positive view of inflation as a policy for a long time to come. Seen from the American point of view, securing solid academic support for inflation as a policy in other countries could act as insurance against someone suddenly re-establishing a real gold standard where they would have to keep their money supply constant. If a country chose gold over fiat money, it could spill over to other countries and eventually make it impossible for the US to export its inflation.

We can summarize this as follows:

- Rockefeller was a significant player in the American banking industry
- Rockefeller's bankers worked to set up a central bank in the United States, which was important for the United States to pursue a centralized expansionary monetary policy
- the US then pursued an expansionary monetary policy leading up to the crash of 1929
- Rockefeller financed a foundation that worked to change economists' methods internationally and facilitate active social management
- the foundation financed Frisch's research stay in the USA
- Frisch established close ties with Professor Irving Fisher, who was central to the development of inflation as a policy in the United States
- Frisch was convinced that inflation was good, and that social development should be controlled
- the foundation financially supported Frisch at the University of Oslo
- the foundation financed dozens of employees who worked for Frisch
- immediately after Frisch took up his position as professor, he began to influence Norwegian politicians in order to gain support for Norway's pursuit of an expansive monetary policy
- the professional development under Frisch was radical, quasi-scientific, and influenced by the fact that he was blinded by the lies of the Soviet Union's propaganda apparatus
- Frisch trained the economists who staffed three of the most important government institutions
- according to journalists and political scientists, these institutions had the blueprints of economic policy in Norway in the palm of their hands
- a number of other economics institutes at European universities also received extensive support from the foundation

In his article, Seim points out that historians have disagreed about whether the Rockefeller Foundation engaged in pure philanthropy or whether they tried to influence the institutes to promote Rockefeller's financial interests. This is something that it is not necessary for us to decide one way or another. Most importantly, the financial support enabled Frisch and his associates to influence politicians to pursue an inflation policy, which in turn helped to make it easier for the United States to do the very same.

**The Austrian School**

Carl Menger was eventually regarded as the architect of the development of the Austrian school. This school had deep roots in the classical tradition in economics and argued for free markets and the protection of property rights. Trygve J.B. Hoff, whom we touched upon with respect to the connection with Lenin's use of inflation as a weapon, was inspired by the Austrian economists Ludwig von Mises and Friedrich Hayek. In 1947, Hoff founded The Mont Pelerin Society together with von Mises and Hayek, among others. The purpose was to disseminate ideas about the nature of free societies and to promote the idea of decentralized markets as an economic organizing principle.

In 1904, von Mises became a student at the Faculty of Law at the University of Vienna, where he also attended lectures in economics. He later worked in a law firm, became an economic adviser, and later chief economist at the Austrian Chamber of Commerce, before becoming economic adviser to the Chancellor. When the Chancellor was killed by a Nazi agent in 1934, von Mises emigrated to Switzerland where he secured a professorship, before moving to the United States in 1940. He wrote many books on the subjects of economics and political science. In his magnum opus *Human Action: A Treatise on Economics*, which was published in 1949, he emphasized that the subject of economics springs from the recognition that:

- every action has a consequence (*causality*)
- human actions are *purposeful*
- the means that man can use to achieve his goals are limited by the *scarcity* of resources
- the future is characterized by *uncertainty*
- valuation of goods is *subjective*
- valuing getting something, such as money, today instead of later (*time preference*) is also subjective

Within the Austrian school, this is held up as an important part of von Mises's work with respect to the restructuring of the classical subject of economics.

Hayek studied law and economics at the University of Vienna, meeting von Mises who eventually became his mentor. He obtained his doctorate in law in 1921, the same in political science in 1923. In 1927, von Mises and Hayek founded the Austrian Institute of Economic Research, which today is the largest within the field of economics in Austria. Hayek headed the institute before being offered a position as professor of economics and statistics at the London School of Economics, a post he held for 18 years.

Hayek worked a great deal with monetary theory and the cyclical fluctuations in the economy. He also wrote extensively on entrepreneurship. He showed that the entrepreneur never has perfect information, that trial and error is a discovery process that plays a central role for economic progress in society through what we call innovation, and that this is not possible within a system based on central planning. Hayek's analysis of this went straight to the heart of what was the problem with the planned economy, Keynes' theories and the Oslo School models, and why Statistics Norway was unable to explain the economic growth when they assessed the development after the Second World War in the 1965 article that we referred to earlier. He also wrote the bestseller *The Road to Serfdom* in 1944, which shows, among other things, how a totalitarian dictatorship develops in democratic societies, such as in Germany after the First World War.

Hoff received his cand. oecon degree, equivalent to a master's degree in economics, in 1916 and later studied economics at Harvard University in the USA. In 1935 he bought the journal Farmand, where he became editor, a position he held until his death in 1982. Hoff was one of the country's foremost champions of free societies, fought hard against most forms of public intervention and had a lot of contact with Hayek.

Aschehoug publishing house published Hoff's book *Economic calculation in socialist societies* in 1938. He had made a critical review of practically everything that had been written in German and English about planned economy, concluded that a socialist economic system was possible, but that it could only work at a low level with regards to production and consumption. The book was critically well-received, including the Economic Journal and the American Economic Review, and subsequently the publishing rights for a French and English edition were sold in 1939.

Frisch encouraged Hoff to submit the book for consideration for his doctorate. Hoff defended his thesis in front of a packed auditorium in November 1939. Frisch, who was one of the opponents when Hoff presented the thesis, had little else to criticize the book for other than that it should have been supported by mathematics, but Frisch dominated the disputation so much that the chairman had to intervene and interrupt him.

In the article Trygve J.B. Hoff: the authorship from 2019, Lars Peder Nordbakken writes that:

> Hoff consistently argued for a stable and politically independent monetary system, balanced public finances, a free market economy, free trade and international economic liberalization

In short, Frisch and Hoff had diametrically different views on both subjects and politics, including when it came to monetary policy.

Those who identified themselves as being part of the Austrian school believed that society does not benefit from having a system where someone actively expands the money supply. On the contrary, they believed that it leads to redistribution of wealth and malinvestments, that it creates market bubbles that will inevitably burst and that the theory of the positive effect of inflation was quite frankly dangerous. They went further than that, with several factions clearly expressing their opinion that this was government-organized fraud, logically concluding, like other forms of fraud, it was completely unethical. This is consistent with what the history of inflation policy has so far taught us quite unequivocally, as explored in the previous chapter.

Von Mises and Hayek refuted other economists' arguments that inflation will lead to increased investment that contributes to economic growth by showing that you cannot get something of economic value out of nothing. Furthermore, they pointed out that one cannot prove that at a given time there is such a thing as an investment level which is optimal for an entire nation. The value of investment was, as with financial goods in general, something that was subjective, and which, among other things, would depend on each individual's time preference and view of risk. Objectively, it will also vary a lot from company to company whether it is deemed to be profitable to invest, when it is right to do so and how much to invest. This is something that a skilled business manager and a competent board can consider for their company. We can take an example to show how such assessments can be reflected in a group that consists of a holding company at the top, further comprising three subsidiaries:

The management's assessment may be that it is right for one subsidiary to increase investment, because it has skilled personnel, and they make quality clothing with a clothing brand that has become very popular. In the second company, which is successful in furniture sales, the group management knows that there they have not found the right manager to be able to scale the company for growth, for example by opening branches of their stores in several cities. In the third company, operations are good and as profitable as they can be, but the product that they sell, CDs, is being swallowed by new technology. For the latter two subsidiaries, it is thus also currently completely out of the question to invest more.

One can go through the same analysis at sector level:

A skilled investor has information that says that too little is being invested in the agricultural sector, and that there is a risk of food shortages if larger areas are not cultivated. At the same time, he sees that too much is invested in social media and in the entertainment industry in general. Therefore, he sees the most upside in food production and the most downside in entertainment. He decides to invest his money in a company that makes small and medium-sized ploughs and sowing machines of good quality at a competitive price.

What happens to these companies and sectors if the governor of the central bank appears on the TV screen and says that the interest rate must now be reduced by half a percentage point? This is the same as announcing that, "now everyone must hurry to borrow and invest a lot more”. For the management group in our example, such news would simply be injurious. They know that when it becomes "free" to borrow money, their companies will also have no choice but to borrow more money and invest in something new if they are to succeed in the competition with a host of new challengers who finance their venture with loans. Alternatively, they could sell some of the subsidiaries to newcomers who are less capable of running a company of that size, but who are proficient at obtaining cheap financing.

This will also be bad news for the investor who invested his capital in the company that manufactures ploughs and sowing machines. He knows that the social media and TV entertainment industries attract investors who are largely financed with borrowed money. He also knows that these companies continuously use this money to draw labor and other resources away from the other sectors, including the agricultural sector. The fewer people who can bear to continue as farmers, the larger the farms will become and the less demand there will be for small and medium-sized ploughs and sowing machines.

The economists of the Austrian school also understood very well what happens when the state begins to control society through monetary policy. A "social engineer", as Ruml called it, who gets control of monetary policy, does not care that there are large individual differences between companies and between sectors. To him it does not matter that the price of money (the interest rate) interferes directly with the market's ability to ensure that the resources flow to the companies and sectors that can meet society's needs in the best possible way. The social engineer may understand that what he is doing has such consequences, but also knows that there are others who must correct unintended negative side effects. For example, by a bureaucrat in the Ministry of Agriculture being tasked with correcting the problem by issuing compensatory monetary grants to those who own the smallest farms.

In this way, intervention in the market's most important medium, which is to say, dictating the price of money, triggers a domino effect. In this scenario there is no end to how many social engineers one must have.

You have the same problem with the fact that there are big differences between the member countries in monetary unions. When all the countries are to have the same key interest rate, it will turn out differently for member countries with different economic situations, which this quote from an article of July 20th, 2022, by journalist Martin Hagh Høgseth on *e24.no* illustrates:

> The economic situation is different in the various countries in the Eurozone. This makes it difficult to set an interest rate that is "suitable for everyone" and the European Central Bank has to compromise with some of the countries.
>
> Germany is one of the most important countries in the euro cooperation and has had good economic development. The German ten-year interest rate is central in the EU and was around 2.25% on Tuesday.
>
> On the other hand, countries such as Italy and Greece have very high national debt. They are therefore very vulnerable to the expected interest rate hike by the European Central Bank. According to a publication from Eurostat, the total debt in EU member states amounted to 93% of the countries' combined gross domestic product in 2021.

The United States and other federal republics have the same problem. For example, an interest rate that is too high for Texas may be too low for Alaska. The same considerations are equally relevant for assessing economic differences within nation states. In Norway, for example, there are big differences between the economic situation in the villages of Trøndelag, in the middle part of country, and in big cities like Oslo in the south.

Von Mises and Hayek also pointed out that if the speculators are to invest more, then the resources that go into increased investment must necessarily be taken from elsewhere in the economy. They showed that if you are to stimulate the general level of investment, then you must necessarily reduce the general level of consumption. This conclusion was a result of the deductive method. What von Mises and Hayek proved would happen was exactly what also happened in Norway when the planned economy that Frisch recommended was seriously put in place after the Second World War. In their article *Ragnar Frisch and the postwar Norwegian economy*, Sæther and Eriksen discussed the paradox that in the post-war period Norway had a significantly higher level of investment than other Western countries, but that economic growth nevertheless lagged, which also had a negative impact on consumption:

> The price for the high investment ratios in Norway in the 1950s and 1960s was a lower rate of growth in private and public consumption.

Von Mises and Hayek explained that politically created stimulation through expansionary monetary policy leads to a reallocation of resources away from:

- production of goods and services with short production lines, i.e., there are short and few chains between a person investing something, via production and until the end user receives the product or service to:

- production of goods and services with long production lines, that is, there are long and many chains between a person investing something, via production and until the end user receives the product or service.

The consequence of shifting investments from short to long production lines is, among other things, a production system where everything tends to become larger and more complex. An example of this is the rise of Gigafactories that are constructed far away from both the raw materials needed to produce the goods, and also far away from those who will buy the final product. Another example is the industrialization of agriculture, which has gone hand in hand with the act of farm properties constantly merging, meaning that farms have become larger in scale but fewer in number.

In short, the production lays claim to more resources, especially capital. The real economy "makes up" for this by moving resources away from consumption, i.e., the opportunity to consume decreases, which is the opposite of what should happen when you stimulate investment according to the theories advocated by the Keynesians and the Oslo School.

The economists from the Austrian school also made important contributions to the understanding of the so-called *business cycle* in the economy – the fluctuations between booms and busts. They showed that expansion of the money supply created an illusion of economic growth. It made companies start up demanding projects that took a long time to complete. As the projects progressed, they realized that there was an increasing scarcity of resources that they need, with a corresponding rise in prices, making it difficult for them to complete the plans. "Everyone" wanted to get hold of the same materials and specialists. The "cheap money" caused widespread malinvestment and speculation, which was bound to be replaced by a period of what people experienced as an economic crisis. This is a very relevant topic today, which we will look at in more detail in the chapter on money's journey.

It is an understatement to say that the views of the economists of the Austrian school on inflation did not go down well with the financial elite, throughout academic nor among the political classes. Von Mises is widely considered to be the most important economist in the Austrian school, but in the United States it proved difficult for him to secure paid work at the universities. He received funding from private benefactors so that he may support his family. *New York University* gave him an unpaid position as visiting professor, which gave him the opportunity to teach students in economics. In the biography Mises – The Last Knight of Liberalism, Jörg Guido Hülsmann writes the following about him: "The colleges and universities shunned him. The political parties in power did not listen and were certainly glad that nobody else seemed to do so either."

The way in which Hoff was treated by academia in Norway has similarities to the way von Mises was treated in the USA. In the 2005 article *The Forgotten Dissertation*, Professor Tore Jørgen Hanisch and Professor Arild Sæther wrote about Hoff's book *Economic calculation in socialist societies* that:

> [His book] could have become an international standard work and which, in our opinion, should have become one in Norway. This was confirmed by Don Lavoie in 1985: "To date, the best overall summary in English of the debate from this alternative perspective is Hoff".

In the article, they discussed the reasons as to why the book had such little influence in Norway and why ultimately his thesis was forgotten. They write:

> Last but not least, Frisch was very skeptical of the free or decentralized market economy that Hoff recommended. It had, as Frisch saw it, broken down during the crises of the interwar period, and the advantages of economic planning as an alternative or supplement to the capricious whims of the market could therefore seem rather obvious. In this sense, it was unnecessary to emphasize alternative perceptions.

Hanisch and Sæther interviewed students who studied at the Department of Economics at the University of Oslo in the post-war years. It turned out that Hoff's views were barely mentioned in the curriculum. Hanisch and Sæther concluded that this was probably as a result of Professor Ragnar Frisch strongly disagreeing with Hoff both in terms of policy and method. The teaching at the economics institute under Frisch has therefore apparently borne the mark of a desire for professional and ideological alignment. After the war, Hoff wrote the books *Peace and the future - the path of liberocracy* in 1945 and *Thoughts and Ideas* in 1975.

In 1950, Hayek emigrated to the United States where he obtained the post of professor in The Committee on Social Thought at the University of Chicago, a role in which he worked on interdisciplinary issues. In 1962 he emigrated to Germany where he became a professor of economic policy at the University of Freiburg.

Murray Rothbard received his doctorate in economics in 1956 at Columbia University in New York. He attended von Mises' open seminars at New York University and was strongly influenced by his work, which in no way made it easy for him to get a job in academia. For a time, he had a permanent position teaching engineering students at the Brooklyn Polytechnic Institute.

Rothbard sustained himself for a long time on private grants, and wrote many books in the fields of history, economics and politics. His book *Man, Economy and State* from 1962 was a further development of von Mises' *Human Action*, where Rothbard emphasized clarifying and simplifying the presentation. In 1963 he wrote the book *What has government done to our money?* whereupon he explained in detail both how the fiat money system and money systems without government intervention work. Rothbard was 60 years old before he received a professorship at the University of Nevada in 1985.

**The Monetarists of the Chicago School**

The Monetarist School sprung from Chicago University in the post-war period. Like the Keynesians, they assumed that economic policy recommendations had to be supported by empirical analysis. They also agreed with the Keynesians that falling prices were bad for economic development and believed that the state had to ensure that the money supply expanded.

The abiding difference between the monetarists and the Keynesians lay with the fact that the monetarists believed that public measures to spend money, i.e., fiscal policy, were not a good way to ensure stable economic development. As long as the government pursued a sensible monetary policy, the market would take care of the rest. Despite the fact that the monetarists argued that the state should control the money supply, they were considered to be *free market economists*, who stood in a kind of opposition to the Keynesians and the Oslo School.

Professor of economics at the University of Chicago, Milton Friedman, is the most famous monetarist. Friedman admired Irving Fisher and said he was the greatest economist the United States has ever had. In 1963, Friedman and Anna Schwartz published the book *A Monetary History of the United States, 1867-1960*, in which they argued that the money supply should increase by 3% per year.

The monetarists supported the US government's decision in 1971 to break its promise with respect to the exchange of dollars for gold. They believed that a pure fiat money system could supply better stability and predicted that the price of gold would fall from the fixed rate of 35 to 10 USD per ounce, corresponding to an assumed value whereupon gold was used only in industry. However, the monetarists' credibility was dealt a blow when, in 1973, the gold price instead jumped to 125 USD per ounce. Latterly it has never dropped below 35 USD and at the time of writing (8 August 2022) it sits at approx. 1,790 USD per ounce.

Alan Greenspan, who was formerly the head of the US central bank from 1987 to 2006, was also a monetarist. Albert Edwards, who at that time was hailed as the world's best stock strategist, famously called Greenspan an "economic war criminal" and advocated prosecuting him for masterminding the dollar expansion that led to the 2008 financial crisis.

**The stagflation that wrecked the theories**

In the 1970s, as mentioned, a sustained and deep economic downturn occurred, due to a combination of rising prices and unemployment. This was not supposed to be a possibility according to the Keynesians and Oslo School theories, which postulated that prices would fall in times of economic decline. The fact that they did not get out of the economic downturn by expanding the money supply and thereby expanding the prices weakened their reputation, both in academia and among the political classes.

**The Nobel Prize**

In 1968, the world's oldest central bank, Sweden's Riksbank, decided upon its 300th anniversary, to create a prize in memory of Alfred Nobel. The prize was to be awarded to economists who had made important and lasting contributions within their field. Frisch received the award in 1969 and Hayek in 1974. It is worth noting then that one of the greatest advocates of expansion of the money supply received the award before Nixon's abolition of the gold standard hastening the onset of stagflation, while similarly one of the greatest opponents of inflation as a policy received the award afterward.

In his Nobel prize lecture, Hayek was anything but gracious in his comments regarding economists who had been the professional alibis for a world relentlessly pursuing a conscious policy of inflation. He charged that his colleagues had full and complete responsibility for the crisis that the world found itself in in the 1970s. Without naming names, Hayek was also critical of economists' attempts to mix empiricism and methodological use from the natural sciences into the subject of economics. Hayek's speech was a verbal dagger thrust in the direction of those who had sown the seeds of the classical tradition's demise.

Hayek's attack was injurious but fell short of becoming the killing blow. The states' dependence on the benefits of expanding the money supply was too great for them to be willing to give it up. Afterall, political elites had systematically used inflation as a policy for almost 2,500 years. The rise of a financial elite that had become reliant on seeing a society hooked on credit probably did not make it any easier for the politicians to wean themselves off inflation as a policy.

When the monetarist Milton Friedman and the Keynesian James Tobin received the Nobel Prize in 1976 and 1981 respectively, it could be deduced that the political balance in the academic discussion about inflation had been restored.

**What economics students learn about inflation today**

Looking at what those scholars at the various economics institutes think about inflation today, it might be instructive to look at the syllabus for those studying the subject in Trondheim where Harald Hardråde augmented his inflation scheme in 1050. Professor Leiv Opstad has written the book *Introduction to Macroeconomics*, which is on the recommended reading list for students at the School of Economics at NTNU. In chapter 11.5, Opstad writes about the *Benefits of inflation*:

> Seigniorage:
>
> The authorities can print money to pay for their expenses. You don't have to pay interest for this benefit, unlike when taking out a loan. This is called seigniorage. The greater the amount of money in circulation, the greater the profit for the money issuer. In a situation where the public sector is struggling with a large debt and has difficulty getting out of it, there is always a way out in using the money printing press.
>
> Great monetary policy freedom of action:
>
> In a country with significant inflation and thus also a high nominal interest rate, the central bank has great freedom of action. If the situation calls for it, the country may have a significant negative real interest rate...
>
> Advantage of money illusion:
>
> The fact that many people are deceived by nominal numbers instead of real numbers can also offer advantages. The authorities can thus collect more tax by not adjusting the tax rates for inflation. Thus, they can change the tax level without getting protests from the taxpayers.

Opstad goes on to write that it is advantageous that the workers do not understand their fall in wages, and that the illusion of money therefore facilitates restructuring in the marketplace. He addresses here what Keynes postulated, that inflation makes it easier to get cuts in workers' real wages when necessary. Plainly speaking, this means that workers will accept a cut in their real wages, because they do not understand that inflation eats away at the purchasing power of their wage income. They are deceived by what Opstad calls the *money illusion*.

Today, in other words, economics students learn that the most dangerous and unethical aspects of inflation policy are benefits.

# The money’s journey

**Introduction**

In this chapter we take a closer look at, among other things, these questions:

- Who owns the central banks and what is the basis for what they decide about the development of the money supply?
- What happens after the new money is created, and what is the money's journey through society?
- Who gains and who loses from inflation, and what mechanisms influence this?

When we follow the journey of money, we also pick up the thread from the chapter regarding historical developments looking at the mechanisms that have led to the situation we have today. The presentation primarily uses Norway and the US as examples but since the monetary system is the same almost all over the world, the issues we are looking at are largely the same in most countries.

The aim of the chapter is to gain a better understanding of how it affects society by becoming better acquainted with the monetary system that we have today.

**Who owns the central banks?**

It is a stated principle that central banks should be independent so that they are not exposed to influence from politicians, banks, and other external forces. But how independent are they really?

The way central banks are organized is a variable thing. In the US, a system consisting of 12 reserve banks has been established. These are owned by private banks. According to *bankrate.com*, 38 percent of the 8,039 U.S. commercial banks are co-owners. The 12 reserve banks pay dividends to their owners, but it is not those dividends from the central bank system that make banking profitable for them. Those who own shares in central banks cannot sell their shares. The 12 central banks are comprised of a superstructure consisting of a board called the *Board of Governors*. The U.S. President appoints seven members to serve on the board. Of these seven members, the president appoints two who serve as chairperson and vice-chairman, respectively. Additionally, within the superstructure, they have a committee called the *Federal Open Market Committee (FOMC).* It is this Committee that decides monetary policy, i.e., the key policy rate, which helps to regulate the money supply. The seven members of the Board of Governors also serve on this committee, headed by the Chairman of the Board of Directors. In addition, the governor of the Regional Reserve Bank of New York is a permanent member and vice-chairman of the committee. Finally, four governors from the remaining regional reserve banks are members who serve on the committee based on a rotation system.

Of the Federal Reserve's first board of directors, representatives from banks owned by J.P. Morgan made up the majority of the board. Furthermore, Morgan's banker Benjamin Strong became the first governor of the Reserve Bank of New York, a position he held until his death in 1928. According to Rothbard, Strong was the person who had the greatest influence on monetary policy. Both the current central bank governor and several of the governors have previously worked in large banks. For the sake of simplicity, I refer to the US central bank system collectively as the "Federal Reserve".

In Norway things are organized a little differently. We only have one central bank. The Central Bank Act dictates that the state owns Norges Bank and that it has a duty to both inform the Government and report to the Storting (the Norwegian Parliament). It also says the government can instruct the central bank in "extraordinary" situations. Norges Bank consists of an Executive Board appointed by the Government. The Executive Board consists of the central bank governor and the deputy governor. Norges Bank also has what's known as a *Monetary Policy and Financial Stability Committee*. This committee is comprised of the Governor and the Deputy Governor and two other members. Much the same as in the U.S., monetary policy is decided by the Committee. Both the Governor and the Deputy Governor have previously held positions in private banks.

The inherent independence of these banks is open to debate, as is who can influence them the most, and what significance the formal rules actually have in practice. The ownership of these central banks indicates who has the most influence over them. Therefore, in the US, it is in my opinion, likely that the financial elite has the most control over the central bank system, while in Norway it is most likely the state. In the following passage, I have chosen to focus on a government's ability to influence central banks.

**The relationship between the government and the central bank**

The voters' belief of whether the government has contributed to growth or precipitated a recession is a decisive factor for a sitting government's re-election. All incumbent governments also know that raising interest rates when necessary is likely to burst the bubbles, predictably leading to a lost election and inevitable change of government. Therefore, everyone in government is incentivized to convince the central bank to pursue an expansionary monetary policy with low interest rates that can create the illusion of growth encouraging people to increase their borrowing thus heightening the demand for more goods and services.

Perhaps the most infamous example of this lies with what many believed to be outright bullying on the part of President Donald Trump when, during a period from 2019 through the COVID-19 pandemic in 2020, he repeatedly accused Federal Reserve chief Jerome Powell of keeping the policy rate too high. Whether Powell gave in to Trump, we can't say for sure. Unquestionably, Powell pumped more emergency money hitherto unseen in US history when the pandemic broke on the shores of his country.

In Norway, we have detailed information on how the government influenced monetary policy in the 1980s. The Conservatives formed a coalition government with two other parties in 1981. The government wanted interest rates to remain low. Credit growth and the money supply increased considerably leading to a crash in the stock and housing markets in 1987. The publicly appointed commission wrote in the report published in 1998, eleven years after the crash:

> But, the Commission says, the political opposition to resorting to instruments that would translate into higher interest rates was also an obstacle to a more effective monetary policy. In two periods in 1986, Norges Bank was forced to supply substantial liquidity to replace the loss of foreign funding and to keep the interest rate at the government's desired level. In the Commission's view, the substantial supply of liquidity from Norges Bank in 1986 - both through market operations and liquidity loans - must primarily be viewed as a result of the Government's interest rate policy. But Norges Bank should have spoken out more clearly if it disagreed with this policy.

"Market operations" means that the central bank creates emergency money by buying securities from other banks. The report also mentioned that the Ministry of Finance did not report on real credit growth:

> The Commission points out that for several years there was a considerable gap between the credit growth targets presented by the Government and the actual growth. Even though the Ministry had continuous information about the strong credit growth, it failed to propose instruments that might be suitable for implementing the target figures.

This illustrates that at that time we were a million miles away from having independently operated central banks. The consequences of the policies leading up to the crash in 1987 were a many and splintered thing. To curb inflation, Norges Bank chose to raise interest rates considerably, leading to the Norwegian economy experiencing its sharpest downturn since the interwar period. Businesses nationwide entered bankruptcy, unemployment tripled, and households experienced crippling person debt. New Zealand also plunged into recession, which led the government to introduce broad economic reforms in many areas.

Things were marginally better in Germany. With reference to greater independence for the German central bank, changes were introduced in several countries to ensure greater independence for their central banks. The same thing happened in Norway. Norges Bank stated that it had gained greater independence. The central banks can hardly be completely independent. If there is a political majority, politicians can clip the wings of the central banks by introducing legislative changes or change the monetary system, irrespective of the current formal organization. Therefore, we and the central banks must expect that an unwillingness to follow the incumbent government's wishes for low interest rates will be met with sanctions.

**The task of central banks**

The general objectives pursued by the various central banks share commonality. In the United States, Congress has laid down a two-pronged mandate for the Federal Reserve, which will work for maximum employment and stable prices. In Norway, the law stipulates that the purpose of Norges Bank is to maintain monetary stability, promote stability in the financial system alongside the development and maintenance of an efficient and secure payment system. Added to this is the central bank's ongoing contribution to high and stable output and employment.

Central banks can also set more concrete targets or be given a more concrete mandate which details how they should work to achieve their goals. In 2001, the Government's mandate to Norges Bank introduced a monetary policy goal aimed at increasing the consumer price index by 2.5% per year. In 2018, the government changed the mandate adjusting to a new target of two percent. This is in line with the Federal Reserve, which has had the same target since 2012.

Society is producing more and more goods. If the money supply remains constant, the increasing supply of goods will disseminate the money among more goods. Then prices will fall, i.e., money will be worth more. Economists call this *deflation*. If the central bank is to achieve a 2% rise in prices, it will thus have to increase the money supply. The defining characteristic of a central bank is therefore that they increase the supply of money.

**Government loans**

The legislation prohibits the central bank from lending money directly to the government. Instead, the government borrows in the open market. Since the central bank regulates the market interest rate, it can facilitate the government's borrowing by pursuing a low interest rate policy. The central bank can also buy government debt in the secondary market. In this way, the Federal Reserve has paved the way for the US to become the highest-indebted country in the world. Practically speaking, the prohibition against central banks extending loans directly to the government does not dampen governments' ability to finance large budget deficits.

**Four types of money**

As previously mentioned in the introduction, money today is essentially created in four different ways. The way it is created allows us to give them the following collective terms: Cash; deposit money; emergency money for banks; and emergency money for others. What they have in common is that they are universally accepted means of payment and that they are not linked to real values such as gold or silver.

**Cash**

The *first* type is so-called *cash*, defined as banknotes and coins issued by the central bank. This is the only physical means of payment used in society today. It is the central bank that decides how many new notes and coins should be created.

**Bank money**

The *second* type of money is *bank money.* This is the kind of money that we have the most of. It is not the central bank, but the other banks that create bank money. But what exactly is bank money and how do banks create it? Journalist Christer Teigen focused on this in his piece that appeared in the newspaper *Finansavisen* in 2015. He mentioned that 94% of our money supply is bank money, and wrote:

> If you ask an economist about how banks work, the answer is usually that banks lend money that others have saved up, or that the bank itself has taken out in loans and earn money on the difference between lending and borrowing rates.

He wrote that economists believe the bank lends part of the money customers deposit in their accounts, and that the rest of the money is left in the bank as a reserve. Barry, for example, deposits 100,000 USD, after which the bank lends 90,000 to Christer. Barry can withdraw his 100,000, and Christer can withdraw his 90,000, which means that the money supply has now risen from 100,000 to 190,000. Economists refer to this as the *'money multiplier'*.

But that is not quite correct. Finansavisen investigated what leading economists thought about this. They interviewed several of them, hit the books and came up with the following result:

– Professor Erling Steigen at BI admitted that his textbook was old-fashioned

- Professor at Columbia Business School Frederic S. Mishkin's book *Macroeconomics - Policy and Practice*, which had been on the syllabus of Norwegian economics schools for several years, was wrong
- Professor at St. Gallen University Manfred Gärtner's book *Macroeconomics*, used in the business school in Bergen's education of *authorized financial analysts* was wrong
- Professor Rolf Jens Brunstad, one of two professors responsible for the course, did not want to admit that the presentation in the book was wrong

Some of the professors they interviewed had a good grasp of this, and a few textbooks also gave a correct representation.

Journalist Teigen pointed out that the misconceptions were so widespread that many in the banking world were compelled to correct them. He referred to, among other things, the Bank of England, which in 2015 published the article *Money Creation in the Modern Economy*, in which they wrote the following:

> This article explains how, rather than banks lending out deposits that are placed with them, the act of lending creates deposits – the reverse of the sequence typically described in textbooks.

As the article points out, economics students' textbooks stated that it was the customer's deposit (the customer's loan of money to the bank) that was the basis for the subsequent emergence of new money, representing the polar opposite of what happens.

The correct thinking is that *bank money* is created when the bank credits the customer's account with a loan. A bank teller hits buttons on the keyboard, suddenly manifesting new money in society the moment the customers receive the loan on their account.

Is this really the way things work? It's a good question, and for the purposes of this book, it is *the only* question. Professor Brunstad would not accept that this was the case, and when Finansavisen explained that "the bank makes money when it makes a loan – without any of the bank's other accounts being affected", he said:

> No, it's not possible. After all, this would go against all accounting principles.

Brunstad is right in that it runs contrary to all practicable accounting principles. But truth it remains – the dominant type of money is *bank money* created when the bank credits a loan to the customer's account. Thus, the dominant type of money is also what we call *credit.* It's hard for people to accept that this is legitimately the case. Indulge me while I hammer this point home. Deputy Governor Jon Nicolaisen of Norges Bank explained this in his lecture to the Norwegian Academy of Science in 2017:

> When you take out a loan from a bank, the bank deposits the loan into your account. The deposit – the money – is created by the bank when the loan is granted. It doesn't retrieve the money from another person's account, or a vault filled with cash. The money the bank lends you, it has created itself – out of nowhere.

In 2019, special adviser Arne Kloster at Norges Bank wrote an article published on Norges Bank's official blog, which states:

> The bank doesn't have to wait for a deposit from another customer before it can give you the money. It also doesn't transfer a deposit it already has to your account.

Finansavisen also quoted from DNB Markets' report *Where does money come from?* written by senior economist Kyrre Aamdal, which reads:

> The fact that banks generate money through lending activities is the opposite of the common belief that banks lend money that others save, and thus only act as an intermediary... Bank deposits are the bank's debt, and not an asset that can be lent.

The newspaper article concluded by referring to Finansavisen, calling the CFO of one of the banks listed on the Oslo Stock Exchange, who wished to remain anonymous:

- Do you take money from another account in the bank when a customer borrows money?
- No.
- So, you don't lend deposits?
- No, that's not how it works.

It appears that the error pointed out by the Bank of England has now been corrected in the textbooks. The point of this exercise isn't only to show that many of the experts have been unaware of what it is that makes the money supply increase, pulling the wool over the eyes of countless economics students to boot. The most important thing is to show how little awareness there has been in economics as to what inflation *really* is and what in fact leads to inflation.

Now, you may think that banks can make as much money as they want. It's not that simple. Some oversight exists in the form of laws and regulations, while it is also regulated by the market mechanisms, i.e., supply and demand for loans. The most important thing here is the central bank's key policy rate.

Among other things, the statutory rules require that borrowers provide collateral when they take out large loans and how many loans banks can provide with collateral in, for example, real estate. Banks and regulators may decide that loans secured on real estate cannot account for more than 80 percent of the property value. The rules also typically decide how much banks can lend in relation to how much equity banks have on their books. Until 2020, banks were not allowed to lend more than a stated amount more than the reserves in their control. For example, the reserve requirement could be that they were not allowed to lend more than 10 times what was in the reserve accounts. The Federal reserve removed this requirement at the outbreak of the COVID-19 in March 2020. Norges Bank quickly did the same, and while the European Central Bank (ECB) requires that banks should have a minimum of 1% reserves, most central banks today have no such requirement.

With respect to the market's way of regulating growth of the money supply, customer demand depends on how expensive it is to borrow, i.e., how high an interest rate they must pay. With high interest rates, customers will borrow less than if they carried lower interest rates. A high interest rate then means that the money supply grows more slowly. Similarly, low interest rates mean that the money supply is growing faster.

When central banks raise the key policy rate, the banks raise the interest rate that their loan customers must pay, thereby reducing customers' demand for new loans, which again reduces the supply of bank money as well as the growth in the money supply. Lowering the key policy rate has the opposite effect. In this manner the central banks set the pace and volume of the other banks' lending.

Considering the supply portion of the loan markets, banks must consider the costs involved in lending money. An example of this is when a customers defaults on a loan due to bankruptcy proceedings, and the bank does not have sufficient collateral for the loan. It is primarily the owners of the bank who must take the loss. Another example is when customers transfer money from their account as payment to an account with another bank. In broad terms, the regulations imply that the bank is obliged either to attract similar deposits, increase equity, sell loan portfolios, or borrow money themselves – and all of these alternatives are a cost for the bank. The more the bank lends, the greater the costs for the bank, which therefore limits lending growth.

When it comes to the instruments used by the government to expand the amount of bank money, **the big picture** is the following:

- The government allows banks to make money out of nothing when they give loans

- The central bank coordinates growth in bank lending and thereby the money supply by setting *the key interest rate*, which in turn decides the banks' lending rates

Bank money disappears when the customers pay back principals on their loans. In a year, banks lend more money than customers pay down. Therefore, the money supply grows incrementally over time.

**Emergency money for banks**

The *third* type of money derives from central banks supplying *emergency money to banks*. If central banks believe that banks are in financial trouble, they can help them by supplying loans carrying shorter or longer repayment periods, or by purchasing securities from them, such as stocks and bonds. When central banks 'print' money that it gives to banks, they are in practice acting as a bankruptcy insurance company for those banks. By saving the banks in this way, they also indirectly become a bankruptcy insurance company for large bank customers, typically listed companies, who depend on getting a steady flow of credit from the banks.

Central banks can also purchase government bonds, or put another way, loans that governments have raised. This is called *quantitative easing*. Central banks buy government bonds in the open market. The sellers are banks and others who have bought government bonds as an investment.

Central banks are using emergency money to push down lending rates. They are trying to get banks to lend more money on loans with long maturities, forcing companies to borrow more money. The idea behind this is that it will force both companies and others to spend and invest more, and that this will lead to "the wheels of the economy turning again". *As we can see, the system is based on the fundamental idea that producing more money and stimulating more borrowing will result in growth in the real economy*.

In recent years, the Federal Reserve has made extensive use of many types of direct market support, including quantitative easing, but this came to a halt on March 9th, 2022. Norges Bank has interfered in financial markets by extending loans with long maturities to banks at the beginning of the financial crisis in 2008, for instance.

When central banks purchase securities with newly created money, the securities appear as assets in their accounts. If they later start selling the securities, they sell them for money, and the money they then receive as payment disappears from society, in the same way as if borrowers pay down their mortgage. Central banks' sale of securities, known as *quantitative tapering*, therefore reduces the money supply.

**Emergency money for others – helicopter money**

The *fourth* and final type is emergency money for others, known as helicopter money. This is a form of social security to citizens, businesses, and institutions within the public sector. The central banks create new money which they give to the state. The governments hand it out to individuals, business entities and other organizations. This is something that may occur if governments believe that there is an emergency situation in society at large. The reason it is called "helicopter money" is due to the fact that it works almost as if you're emptying buckets of money over the landmass out of helicopters.

The stated goal of helicopter money is to get people to spend more money, based on a theory that companies will then start producing more and hiring more people. We have covered what the real effect of such a policy is when we explored the concept of the *quantity paradox.*

Central banks rarely use this instrument, but many did so during the COVID-19 pandemic, when they *"printed"* money and allowed states to distribute it to businesses and the population. However, the money was not evenly distributed. The general trend was that the largest companies received a relatively larger share of the newly created money than small companies, while still other companies were not qualified at all. This probably led to a substantial redistribution of resources in the real economy.

**The banks**

Anyone who wants to open a bank must apply for a license from the financial authorities. The regulations impose a host of requirements on the licensees. The applicant must employ personnel who possess the relevant professional competencies as well as sufficient seed money. In Norway, for example, the minimum requirement is EUR 5 million. The person granted a license is subject to strict regulations. All countries have one or more supervisory body that are responsible for ensuring that banks do not contravene the rules.

**Consumer price index**

The Consumer Price Index (*CPI*) is more commonly understood to be the *cost of living index*. It should reflect the price changes in the previous 12 months for goods and services that a private household consumes. All states have someone who analyzes price developments and publishes statistics. In the United States, this institution is called the U.S. Bureau of Labor Statistics. In Norway, that body is Statistics Norway.

In addition to the central bank regulating the interest rate based on a target of rising CPI by 2% per year, CPI is used for many other purposes in society, including:

- regulation of public social security benefits

- regulation of pension benefits, both public and private
- conversion of nominal prices/values to real values, e.g., real GDP
- regulation of leases (for example rent contracts)
- regulation of salaries
- regulation of prices in business practices

Since the CPI both forms the basis for setting the central bank's key policy rate and decides the regulation of other highly significant costs in society, the setting of the CPI is much more important than the central bank's setting of the key policy rate.

The main problem with the CPI it is only *one number*, while everyone's cost of living varies widely. There are big differences from person to person, depending on age, place of residence, income level, interests, and priorities, to name but a few.

Electricity prices serve as a good example. In Norway we have low transmission capacity from North Norway to South Norway. The prices in the spot market were historically almost the same in the two regions. In November 2020 the publicly owned utility company Statnett started exporting electricity to Germany and the UK via two new cables from South Norway. Prices exploded in the south, while they remained unchanged up north. For instance, in November 2021 the price difference was 3:1.

Another problem is that the agencies have a huge opportunity to exercise discretion when they set the CPI. A car cost perhaps 220,000 NOK in 2015, while the same model costs 320,000 NOK in 2022. They may make deductions from price increases at their discretion, citing that there has been a quality improvement during the period, for example with the new model having better safety equipment or using less electricity. It is very difficult to verify whether such discretionary assessments are objectively correct.

It is also obvious that the authorities have strong incentives to underreport developments in the cost of living. With a low increase in the CPI, expenditure on government employees, pensioners and social security recipients will be lower.

The conclusion is therefore that it remains difficult to discuss whether the CPI is *correct* or not. It is probably better to acknowledge that it is a political tool for the government.

In the US, the CPI rose steadily over the past year, from 5.3% in August 2021 to 9.1% in June 2022. In the same period the consumer price index in Norway rose by 6.3%. This is as a result of the growth in the money supply was enormous in the period 2020 to 2021 in both countries. In practice, the central banks threw the mandate of annual inflation of two percent on the fire when the COVID-19 pandemic hit. Many of the other central banks followed the same path.

**Legalised cartels**

The central bank's coordination of the banks' loan rate and the volume of their lending is the same as coordinating the price of a commodity and the total quantity of the commodities offered in a marketplace in the real economy. This means that banks make up what we call a *cartel*. It makes the banking business a special case. In most other industries, coordinating the price of the most important commodity and the quantity of goods that companies sell will result in a violation of competition law that can lead to serious criminal convictions. In the banking industry, this is not illegal. Quite the contrary, the business is organized in this way through legislative means. Banks are therefore *compulsory cartels established by law*.

**How banks earn money**

Banks earn their money, among other things, on interest and fees paid by loan customers. In other words, they make money by lending something that they don't in reality have themselves. Banks are therefore *the group* in society that benefits *directly* from monetary policy. They have simply been granted a license to "print" electronic money. And the greater the lending volume, the higher their income – if the customers can repay. Magne Geber writes in his 2019 master's thesis *The art of creating money in the modern economy* that he has calculated that Norwegian banks' total earnings due to money creation are between 0.54 and 0.95% of GDP.

Banks are also involved in many other forms of financial services. They manage mutual funds and access investment opportunities themselves, both with their own money and borrowed money. However, the basis of the business is the privileged status they have, in that they create new money and have income from this money via their lending practices.

**Borrowers**

Immediately after the customers have signed the loan papers, the money is in their account. Customers use the newly created money to buy more or less valuable assets. What was just *nothing* is "transformed" into, for example, a car, a house, a factory, or stocks.

It is the customers who can take out the largest loans who receive the greatest benefits. They are always incorporated as limited liability companies, and they borrow as much as they can. Other customers also want to borrow large sums of money. However, there is a limit to how much risk they can take, how adequate the collateral they provide as a guarantee for borrowing and the ability they have to repay the loans. This means that banks are not willing to lend them as much money.

**Competing Purchasing Power**

The borrower's money is a credit-generated purchasing power. This competes with money that represents a purchasing power created with real economic values such as labor, real estate, and capital. The more the money supply grows, the more the purchasing power from borrowed money outcompetes the purchasing power of money from value creation in the real economy.

**The largest magnet**

The difference in how much you can borrow means absolutely everything. One customer may be able to borrow enough money to buy a cabin from a company that owns a huge forest property, while the other can borrow enough money both to buy the company and to build 50 new cabins in the forest. The newly created money is like a magnet that attracts real economic value. Whoever can take out the largest loan has the biggest magnet.

**New money is put into circulation**

As the new money is put into circulation, i.e., when borrowers make a purchase, prices will rise. They rise because there is new money that has not been in circulation before which represents a demand that didn't exist previously. However, *a general price inflation is a gradual process that takes time*. One can imagine the following:

- A businessman takes out a loan as soon as the banks open on January 2nd. When he is credited with the loan on his account, he uses part of the newly created money right away to buy a farm, because he plans to develop the property into a new housing estate
- His payment is transferred to the real estate agent on January 3rd. The agent sits on the money until the property is transferred to the businessman, and on February 1st, the agent deposits the money into the farmer's account
- The farmer uses the money to buy a newly built apartment from a real estate company in Oslo. On February 2nd, he transfers the money to another agent's account. Then another month passes before the settlement is ready. On March 1st, the real estate company receives the money in its account
- The real estate company has decided that shareholders will receive dividends, but it will not be paid until May 15th. The general manager owns shares, and she receives NOK 1 million after tax. She saves the money until she helps her son to buy an apartment. He is currently on compulsory military service, and they wait to find an apartment until they know where he will live afterwards

- In October, he learns that he has been accepted to the University of Oslo, and just before Christmas they find a suitable apartment. On December 31st, she transfers the money that her son receives as equity to the agent's account

In this example, in the preceding year, the price of the apartment in Oslo has increased by 10%. By comparison, the deposit rate has been minimal due to expansionary monetary policy. Thus, purchasing power, measured against the cost of entering the housing market, has weakened by 10% from the time the businessman was allowed to borrow the money from the bank at the start of the year until her son buys the apartment. If the farmer who sold the farm to the businessman had instead deposited the money in a savings account and rented a home, the lost purchasing power that his money had gained over a longer period of time would have been halved within 7 years, when measured against 10% annual price increase in housing.

**The time factor is crucial**

While prices of real estate and securities in the financial market rise rapidly as soon as the new money begins to flow, prices on other goods rise more slowly, as many businesspeople and other bank customers' newly created money gradually works its way through society. The reason being? It takes time from the moment the new money is injected via real estate and financial markets until it has percolated through to the real economy.

The deeper new money penetrates the real economy, it must also be distributed among a myriad of goods and services, compared to the relatively more concentrated assets found in the real estate and securities markets. Therefore, the average percentage rise in prices is not as high in the rest of the real economy, for food, clothing, and other mass-produced goods, for example.

At the lower section of economic goods sits raw materials, which in volume and quantity are enormous in number. The new money is spread amongst a large number of goods that in percentage terms are even less affected than finished consumer goods. The general trend will be that commodity prices increase very little when compared with real estate and securities. For instance, global prices for wheat, corn, soy, oats and coffee were about the same in 1975 as in 2005. It is therefore no coincidence that commodity producers like farmers are one of the groups that lose the most in a society plagued by inflation.

Richard Cantillon was an Irish economist who in 1755 was the first to describe the importance of time when related to the flow of money. The *Cantillon effect* implies that the first recipients of money benefit at the expense of those who receive the money last. In practice this acts as a taxation of the latter group, where the recipients of the tax are those who are in the former group. Cantillon was a banker and collaborated with John Law on the creation of the Banque General, taking part as he did in the speculation of the Mississippi Company. He observed firsthand what happened to the prices in France.

**Which prices increase the most**

An important reason as to why prices of property and securities rise first and to a greater extent lies in the knowledge that these assets are well suited for purchases via debt financing.

With respect to securities, it is primarily those securities listed on the stock exchange, particularly easy-to-sell stocks, and bonds in large companies, that respond to the expansion of the money supply. The opportunity to buy shares with borrowed money gives the large companies a competitive advantage, comparable to the effect that a steroid will have on an athlete. Lending fiat money contributes to inflated share prices, which in turn leads to companies receiving relatively higher prices per share if they want to finance their business by issuing new shares. With the money the company receives by selling new shares they can use it to buy or build a modern factory that increases their competitiveness in the marketplace, for example.

Such advantages for large companies produce a corresponding handicap for small unlisted companies who compete in the same market. The effect over time is that the big companies become increasingly dominant whilst smaller companies grow ever smaller and less profitable. This is typically seen in the big cities. Today, most major cities look the same. It is the large retail and restaurant chains that dominate. You don't have to look farther back than the 1980s and 1990s to see that the landscape was completely different, with many different independent shops and restaurants.

Real estate is similarly a suitable solution for debt financing. However, there are some properties that provide banks with better security than others. Some areas are also more valuable due to demand and scarcity. Simply put location, location, location. Homes with a sea-view, proximity to amenities and transport links are illustrative here. Some property types, such as apartments, are in general easier to sell quickly than other property types. Therefore, apartments in larger cities, where values are generally higher and turnover is faster than elsewhere, will fit the bill as collateral for loans. The same effect occurs as with listed shares in large companies, in that inflation gives apartments in the big cities a competitive advantage compared to properties with detached houses in rural areas, for example.

**The money multiplier**

As we saw, Christer Teigen of Finansavisen wrote that several leading economists did not know how new money is created. In the article, he also wrote that it has been common to believe that the combination of bank deposits and lending has a 'money multiplier' effect. It is true that we get such an effect, but it happens in slightly different ways than what people have thought. Below I explain one of these mechanisms:

We can imagine that we have a mini society with 10 people living in separate houses, and that together they have a money supply of 1 million USD that until now has been kept constant. One day Andrea decides to start a bank, *Banco Andrea*, that lends money that she does not have, but which is created when she gives customers loans.

Barry wants to borrow money to buy a tractor and offers Banco Andrea a mortgage on his residential property as collateral for the loan. The property is worth 100.000 and Banco Andrea says he can borrow up to 80% of the value of the house, i.e., 80,000. Barry accepts the bank's offer and buys Christer's tractor with the borrowed money.

Christer has longed to buy Barry's residential property. Previously, he offered to pay 100.000 for the property. After the tractor sale, Christer has more money, so now he offers 110.000. Barry declines again.

Barry needs a plough for his tractor. He asks Banco Andrea for a new loan to buy the plow. The bank says it can still only give Barry a loan of up to 80% of the value of the home, and since the home is now worth 110,000, Barry can borrow 8,000, equivalent to 80% of the 10,000 appreciations of the value of Barry's property.

When Denise, Everett, Francesca, and the other citizens in this mini-society also start taking out loans, residential properties continue to rise in value, because the money supply increases. As the value of Barry's property increases, he can finance more and more of his farm operations, on the basis of loans secured with his property as collateral.

This is a simplified and exaggerated example, but it shows that *money multiplication* is partly a result of inflated values being used as collateral for new loans that provide further expansion of the money supply. This effect, which is like compound interest rates, intensifies over time and becomes greater in markets where debt-financed purchases are common, such as the real estate and securities markets, particularly in areas where turnover is rapid.

The redistributive effect becomes more powerful the longer a fiat money system is allowed to operate without a market crash occurring. The large general increase in house prices in recent years, which is a direct result of the expansion of the money supply, shows this clearly. In Oslo, house prices have roughly doubled in the last ten years. To illustrate a point: Robert is lazy and often unemployed, but in 2012 he received help to buy a three-bedroom apartment in Oslo for 3 million NOK. The purchase price was 80% financed by loans, with his parents standing as guarantors, plus a further 20% as loans from his parents. He sells the apartment in 2022 for 6 million.

After repaying the loans to the bank and parents, he finds himself 3 million in profit, thus his equity. He will use the money to buy a new place to live in Steinkjer, where price points are much lower. Just outside the city, he finds a small farm for sale. A family of four from Malm also wants to buy the small farm. The parents have worked and saved for 20 years, and the entire family has led a frugal life. They've done it that way because they've been taught that debt is bad. They have 2,900,000 in savings, yet Andrew outbids them, as he buys the small farm for 3,000,000. We see here that the purchasing power that Andrew has gained directly because of credit and inflation outcompetes the purchasing power that the family from Malm has gained through hard work and savings.

In other words, you don't have to be a smart real estate investor in the big city to outcompete people in the rural areas when you get help from inflation. It would suffice to find someone who is willing and able to give you a loan and that you can accept living in the hustle and bustle of the city for a few years. Later, you can enjoy life in a free house in a nice place in the provincial regions of Norway. This effect is so well known that it draws many young people into the cities to enter the housing market, in the hope that after a few years they can cash in the inflation profit and move back home to start a family there. However, the places where most of the newly created money enters the economy act as powerful magnets for both labor and capital. As a result, the inflation economy means that migration flows largely from rural areas into the big cities rather than the other way around.

**Low risk – safe investment?**

This system means that the largest borrowers will gain control of an increasing share of society's resources, at the expense of those who work hard and save. If the money supply increases, most prices go up. The general attitude in the financial sector is that those who invest for the long term without taking excessive risk are almost guaranteed a good return. Most people are also of the opinion that debt-financed home purchases are safe investments, which we will return to in the discussion chapter.

**Those who earn the most**

To sum up, those who get hold of the new money first and who get to borrow the most benefit the most from the growth of the money supply. Particularly, it is investors in the real estate and financial markets who benefit from the new money flowing into our economy.

**How the government benefits from the inflation policy**

As we have seen previously, the government will benefit from this system in that it can have the central bank give it everything it needs with respect to loans. In modern times, the government borrows by selling promissory notes more commonly known as government bonds. Central banks also have a practice of buying government bonds in the secondary market. This creates security for banks and others who invest in government debt.

However, a government does not have to take out loans to profit from the system. This is especially true if the government has already managed to increase taxes as much as society can handle, which is the case in Norway. For example, VAT, stamp duty and taxes on fuel and electricity ensure that the government receives a daily flow of the inflated real values traded in the market.

**Other "winners"**

Others can benefit greatly from this monetary policy even without borrowing. This applies primarily to those who own or are managers in companies that are closely linked to those parts of the market where the influx of new money is greatest. The same applies to senior executives in the public sector. In addition, the intermediary companies, especially those engaged in real estate, stock brokerage and facilitation of the sale of securities will profit greatly from it. Therefore, many of the banks also focus on real estate, stock brokerage and a lot of other activity related to securities.

**National economic development**

What can we say about the relationship between inflation as a policy and national economic development?

It is not an easy task to quantify the effect that individual socio-economic and political factors may have on economic growth. There are many factors, and they vary over time because the economy is dynamic. Therefore, this kind of exercise involves a high level of uncertainty.

Almost all prominent economists agree that property rights, respect for contracts and access to the courts are of vital importance to economic development. This means, for instance, that abolition of property rights will be detrimental to economic growth, something which the Soviet Union and other communist countries proved beyond doubt. The Peruvian economist and author of *The Mystery of Capital*, Hernando de Soto, highlights the importance of well-functioning systems for registration of ownership to real estate. Many opine that free international trade and allowing different countries to specialize in areas where they have comparative advantages are of the utmost importance. This has formed much of the basis for the globalist movement within politics. Today, however, we see a tendency where economists and politicians are not as sure about this as they used to be. The Norwegian economist and author of *How Rich Countries Got Rich*, Professor Erik Reinert, is one of them. He argues that a combination of government intervention, protectionism, and strategic investment are the key drivers in a successful development of nations' economies. Former American President Trump and many of his supporters have a similar view.

It is extremely difficult to demonstrate how much inflation may damage some countries' economies or benefit others. **The big picture** is that it has been impossible to prove empirically that nations in general will benefit from inflation, whether we talk about a small or a high degree of inflation.

What we know for sure is that countries with hyperinflation invariably experience economic decline. We also know that some countries earn revenues directly from exporting their inflation. The cost of money production is close to zero, and when other countries accept the money in exchange for goods and services, the revenue stream can be significant. The United States is the best example, and Americans are completely open about the fact that they have this advantage. The New York Times' editorial *America's Most Profitable Export: Money: The world has a growing appetite for small green pieces of paper with Benjamin Franklin on the front*, on March 9th, 2019, is one example. Neither does the Federal Reserve try to hide this fact. In an episode on January 17th, 2021, on the economics podcast The Bob Murphy Show, Federal Reserve Bank of St. Louis economist David Andolfatto elaborated on how important dollar exports are to the United States. Listening to Andolfatto, one gets the impression that the Federal Reserve and its economists are proud because they have managed to strike a balance between income from dollar exports and low domestic price inflation. The interview took place while the Federal Reserve printed an enormous amount of money during the COVID-19 pandemic. It would be interesting to listen to a follow-up interview, now that we know what this expansion of the money supply has done to the economy.

Other countries which benefit from having a popular currency, such as those in the Eurozone, may also earn some revenue from inflation export. The same goes for Japan, the UK and China.

However, it is still difficult to quantify and analyze if the country that exports its' currency has an inflation policy that gives the country a net benefit. The disadvantages may outweigh the advantages, and they will in any case be unevenly distributed among different groups within the country. If one group benefits at the expense of other groups, it is also difficult to argue that the policy is positive for the nation per se.

**The centralization effect**

The combined effect of the help that the government, the financial industry, big businesses, and the real estate market get from stimulating growth in the money supply is a contributing factor in big cities attracting people and capital as if they were giant magnets.

Oslo is a typical example. There we have the parliament, the country's largest courts, the largest concentration of the state's central administration, as well as the financial industry. This means that the influx of new money is significantly greater in Oslo compared to, for example, a remote village in Northern Norway. This means, among other things, that the value of real estate is rising significantly faster in Oslo.

At the same time, homebuilders in Oslo and rural areas in Northern Norway will compete when they buy the same materials for house building. Cement products, painting, fittings, woodwoork, tiles, electrical components, and many other building materials will cost roughly the same regardless of where you live in the country. In Oslo, the builder will typically experience a quick return after building a villa, because the value of the completed house exceeds the construction costs. In the rural areas, the person who sets up a new villa will often find that the construction costs will be higher than the value of the completed house, if it is to be sold immediately afterwards in the secondary market. This means that those who build new villas in rural areas must own the house over a long period before the slow tide of price inflation has lifted the project out of a financial loss and into a moderate nominal positive return. The knowledge that people will not recover the expenses of construction costs if they must sell quickly gives people incentives to move to more central areas.

This has affected three things particularly negatively when related to social and economic conditions which is clearly visible in Norway:

- Farms are closed, grazing areas and cultivated land are overgrown, large farmhouses and old farm buildings are in drastic disrepair, and many new barns are empty
- The rural schools are closed, the school buildings are empty and decaying
- The rural retirement communities are closing and many among the elderly move far away from their homes in their final years

The centralization effect is drastic. The youth demographic and retirement communities disappear, and the villages crumble. It is not only the expansion of the money supply that is the cause. But, unlike any other policy, inflation lies at the very bottom of our economy and society, and functions almost like a slightly sloping funnel. This funnel encourages everything to roll slowly-but-surely to the center. Inflation policy simply creates a fundamental imbalance, that makes it stand out from all other political tools.

**Not even a zero-sum game**

The vast majority will experience the disadvantages of inflation policy. The reason for which is simple: a monetary system that primarily contributes to the redistribution of resources by placing them in the hands of those who take out the most loans cannot, by definition, make everyone rich. It is at best a *zero-sum game*, where some must lose for others to win. The more someone wins, the more someone else loses.

I write here that it is *at best* a zero-sum game, but in reality, it is a game that systematically destroys the benefits of free trade. While the inflation economy is pulling real estate, capital and labor in the direction of those who are best at obtaining credit and keeping as close as possible to the influx of newly created money, free trade causes resources to flow in the direction of those who are good at meeting old and new needs that people have in the fastest way possible, with the least possible use of resources and at the lowest possible cost. Inflation policy therefore leads to a destruction of value and a profligate waste of resources compared to allowing the market to simply do its job. The inflation economy makes society poorer and can be compared to a struggle to use debt as a means to acquire the biggest possible share of a pie that is steadily shrinking.

**The biggest losers**

It is those people not able to take out loans or who refrain from it, and those who are far away from the flow of new money, who lose the most. This includes most ordinary wage earners, including those who work in the public sector, except for senior executives. Everyone must live somewhere, and few of us can or want to be speculators who "flip" homes or buy and sell shares. For this group, which makes up the largest share of citizens, increased house prices will drive up costs of materials and craftsman services, so that expenses for home maintenance rise proportionally. Wage increases to compensate for the rise in the consumer price index are normally not sufficient to compensate for the increased expenses incurred when owning homes that require continuous maintenance. The current cost of living crisis in the UK, but more broadly across Europe, proves that it is about time to scrutinize the CPI as a policy tool.

Pensioners are also a high-risk group with respect to losing out. Many have benefited from inflation eating up their loans, but now there is a real risk that it might also eat up both their pensions and their lifesavings. Inflation has led some of the retirement community to take out loans and increase their consumption. Some take out loans and provide their own home as collateral to "help their children "getting a foot on the property ladder". In Norway, a market has also begun to develop for a new type of loan: *senior loans* or *pensioner loans*, in which people aged 60 and over can receive periodic payments of quasi-*pensions* from the bank, in the form of a loan secured by a mortgage on their home. Once the pensioner has started receiving payments, the debt automatically increases. The reason being that interest is constantly added, and the pensioner pays neither interest nor instalments. The effect of pensioners starting to take out loans and providing guarantees for their children is, among other things, that they take risks in a phase of their life where they absolutely cannot tolerate bad investments. Time is quite-literally not on their side. Furthermore, they have no 'productive years' left to redress the balance if things go wrong.

As previously mentioned, farmers are among those who struggle the most in a society with a lot of inflation. In the period after World War II, Norwegian farmers negotiated directly once a year with the government for subsidies for their work and production. This locks farmers into prices in a planned economic system. It creates a rigidity in addition to farmers' produce being last in line when the new money seeps through the real economy. Farmers in Norway are paid so poorly for their work and end up so far outside the inflation economy that the vast majority have been driven to take out loans to build large production buildings, in turn buying larger, presumably more expensive heavier equipment. An interview with young farmer Yngve Røøyen in Rindal in Norway published on *nationen.no* September 12th, 2022, illustrates the situation well:

> *I know that I am very angry. We invested as the policy allowed, and now we have so much debt and such big costs that I feel tied hand and foot and thrown into deep water. We have no choice but to continue. Had we tried to sell the farm, we probably wouldn't have been left with enough money to cover the debt, says Røøyen...*
>
> *Before I became a farmer, I was a carpenter. When the prices of building materials rise, yes, it becomes more expensive to build houses and cabins. This is also how it is in my snow plowing job. Now that diesel is expensive, plowing becomes more expensive for the customer. As a farmer, we do not have this opportunity, because our prices are determined in the agricultural settlement, says Røøyen.*

I called Røøyen and asked him to sum up the situation the way he sees it. He said:

> *The investment cost for a new cowhouse is twice as large as the increase in value that the property has after the building has been erected and put into use. People who are still farmers today are primarily those who have so much debt that they cannot afford to sell their farms without incurring huge losses. We are locked in.*

In other words, the combination of centralized economic planning and inflation has forced the farming sector to become capital-intensive and heavily indebted while the farms have become fewer in number and larger in scale.

Individuals who buy a home with debt financing are also at risk. If they are unlucky with their timing, they risk becoming the biggest losers in the biggest pyramid scheme in history.

It is possible to free oneself from many of the disadvantages of the inflation economy, but this requires a conscious and active effort. We'll come back to this towards the end of the book.

**The real crisis**

It logically follows that it is during the period when the growth in the money supply takes place and prices are inflated that problems arise, because values are redistributed on such a large scale. *This is the real crisis*. However, as we have seen, the ways in which the central bank and the government handle what happens when the bubbles burst will also have a major impact on how much damage is inflicted on society due to inflation policy, which we will return to soon.

**Blind to the crisis**

Most people don't experience it that way. They are deceived by the paper values that the money illusion creates, such as when homeowners see prices of homes sold in the neighborhood just go up and up. It gives people a feeling that they are only getting richer and richer, and quite a few of them most likely conclude that they must have made a smart "investment". It is more difficult for them to spot the development of the prices of goods and services they individually consume. They just get a general feeling that they have to work more, buy less, or take out more loans to make it work. This is one of the main and abiding reasons why people are increasingly stuck in the debt trap.

**The monetary policy «sweet spot»**

The *equilibrium* that occurs when the banking system maximizes the redistribution of resources without making people and companies so worried that they trigger a crash, can be defined as the "sweet spot" of inflation policy. Seen from the perspective of those who are the recipients of the greatest benefits from the inflation economy, those who are in a position to influence developments, this is reminiscent of the story of how one should proceed if one is going to cook a live frog: One must take care to turn the heat up very slowly! You don't want the frog to figure it out and make a run/jump for it! Frogs, it would appear, aren't as clueless as we humans! They figure it out quickly and are on their bike well before the heat risks their legs ending up on a plate in France.

We have looked at the growth in the money supply on several timelines, and it seems that the most common scenario is that the money supply has on average grown by about 7- 8% each year, with higher growth in times of crisis. There is reason to ask if this is a coincidence or if those who benefit the most from inflation policy have known that this is an optimal rate. If one considers money production as a sort of business, it is strange if those who control the money supply aren't fully aware which rate of production provides the most profit over longer periods of time.

**Crash!**

When the growth in the money supply begins to slow, or people notice that the resources in society that are supposed to meet their needs are no longer there to the same extent as before, people usually start to think something has gone a little wobbly.

A steady stream of new money and artificially low interest has led to companies investing in complex production architecture. Some of them reach a point where they realize that there are not enough resources available in the real economy to finalize their project resulting in a profitable business. Cheap money does not build factories. The companies need materials and skilled labor to do this, and resources are precariously scarce.

Banks grow uneasy and less willing to provide new loans. Citizens and businesses do not demand loans to the same extent as before. In this transition phase, typically the interest rates on the so-called *2-year loans* in the money market suddenly become higher than the interest rates on the *10-year loans*. This indicates that banks are suddenly hitting the brakes with respect to their lending. Historically, it turns out that this is something that occurs ahead of an economic downturn or a recession.

If this sounds a lot like musical chairs, you would be right in thinking that, only in this game the chairs do not disappear neatly or sequentially when the music stops. When the penny drops for the masses that the increase in value is just a confection, and that the balloon cannot be infinitely inflated, they do not dare to borrow more money. Instead, people will try to quickly exit the market, sell part of what they've bought and pay off their loans before prices crash and interest rates skyrocket. The professional investors mostly manage it on time, but it's harder for homeowners and amateurs, who have been lured by the low interest rates and the ever-rising prices, to try their hand at speculation or to buy something that carries high costs. Many people find that they are stuck in homes that they cannot afford to live in, and with a debt that gradually exceeds the value of their homes due to falling property prices.

**The «boom and bust» cycle**

As mentioned, the economists of the Austrian School emphasized that expansion of the money supply leads to a period of what is perceived as economic growth - the "boom" - which is always replaced by a period of what is experienced as an economic crisis - the "bust". Furthermore, we saw that highlighted periods of increase in the money supply leads to speculation and unsound investments. We will take a closer look at this, and use Norway as an example, because here the pattern has been absolutely unequivocal. All the crashes that we have had since 1890 came to be because of the expansion of the money supply through credit growth. In the article *Three booms and busts involving banking crises in Norway since the 1890s*, Karsten R. Gerdrup writes:

> *This paper provides a study of three booms and busts involving banking crises in Norway (1899-1905, 1920-1928, and 1988-1993). Financial sector development appears to be closely linked to booms and busts in economic activity during these years. The boom periods that preceded each of the three crises all have some common features: Significant bank expansion, considerable asset price inflation and increased indebtedness.*

The banking crisis in 1920-1928 was followed by a period of high unemployment. From 1935 there was an upturn, which ended abruptly when Germany invaded Norway in 1940. After the liberation in 1945, the government continued several planned economic measures with emphasis on price regulation and rationing of economic goods. At the same time, the government pursued a consistently low interest rate policy which led to an increase in the money supply, in line with the Oslo School's thesis that more money in circulation would lead to increased consumption thus stimulating increased investment. Bank lending increased more than six-fold from 1946 to 1962, while the nominal value of banknotes in circulation more than doubled. Consumer prices tripled in the period from 1938 to 1965.

Price regulation of residential properties meant that there was limited opportunity for homeowners to use their homes as collateral to take out loans that could be used for investment and speculation. This amounted to a kind of brake on credit growth in the private sector. In the 1960s, the government shifted its focus to the regulation and rationing of credit, where the authorities were given the opportunity to dictate which industries should be allowed to take out loans. This to some extent acted as a brake on the growth of the money supply. The fact that the public sector was heavily involved in investment in Norway is a further explanation as to why there were no major crashes in the securities and property markets during this period.

In 1982, the year after the Conservative-led coalition took power, the government took the initiative both to remove price controls and to deregulate the banking industry. This made it easier for banks to offer loans, and people were able to use their homes as collateral for loans to a greater extent than before. Both banks and customers adapted quickly, and the following years were characterized by borrowing secured with homes and other real estate. Debt-financed investments fueled both the stock exchange and the real estate market. The inevitable crash came in 1987, first on the stock exchange and then in the real estate market.

It was triggered by a crash on the New York Stock Exchange, as a direct result of a prolonged expansion of the money supply. According to Murray Rothbard's article from 1988, *Nine myths about the crash*:

> To put it simply: the reason for the crash was the credit boom generated by the double-digit monetary expansion engineered by the Fed in the last several years. For a few years, as always happens in Phase I of an inflation, prices went up less than the monetary inflation. This, the typical euphoric phase of inflation, was the "Reagan miracle" of cheap and abundant money, accompanied by moderate price increases.

Norges Bank and the Norwegian government were afraid that inflation would spiral out of control, so they raised the interest rate. The mortgage rate remained high over several years, and at its peak it was above 15%, while unemployment rose from 2 to 6%. As a result of the measures, real house prices in Norway fell by an average of 42.6% over the five years from 1987 to 1992. Many homeowners lost their entire equity, leading them unwittingly to financial calvary.

Norway's monetary policy after the crash in 1987 had clear parallels with the parity policy of the 1920s, in that the central bank curbed growth in the money supply in society more than ordinary borrowers could withstand. We previously used the example of a borrower who had to repay twice the value of gold in 1928 versus what he had borrowed in 1925. If we run the same exercise and compare the value of money in 1987 and 1992 with the value of real estate, we see that someone who borrowed enough money to buy an apartment in 1987 choosing to repay the loan in 1992, then paid back an amount that was almost enough to buy two such apartments, with the addition of interest. This shows how expensive it was to repay loans when the central bank conducted this monetary policy. There is no surprise that this monetary policy had major adverse effects on the real economy.

When *the average decline* in the housing market was as large as 42.6%, it is clear that the government's *negligent* inflation policy had an effect that began to resemble that which Lenin managed to achieve, when he *intentionally* wiped out almost all of the Russian people's assets during three years of expansion of the money supply.

There are at least two lessons from the crisis in Norway in the 1980s. The first is how little time it can take from gearing up the money supply until the crash is triggered. The second is the extent of the adverse effects if the central bank curbs the growth of the money supply too harshly. Applying the brakes quickly might make sense, but unless the government simultaneously implements measures to mitigate the problems, for example by reducing taxes and the public sector's share of the economy, the real economy will swiftly cut down at the knees. Finally, the crisis will hit ordinary workers and homeowners disproportionately hard.

**Inflating the biggest bubble**

Instead of putting the brakes on full force as the Norwegian central bank did after the crash in 1987, the Federal Reserve, led by Alan Greenspan, chose to give banks so much emergency money that it counteracted the effect of the interest rate hikes, so that the money supply nevertheless continued to rise. Thus, the central bank postponed the correction instead of making it right away. One of the consequences was that prices in the US housing market just levelled off before they began to rise again.

When the dotcom-bubble burst in 2000, the central bank again handled the situation by providing banks with emergency money, and once again after the terrorist attacks on the US September 11th, 2001. Since the turn of the Millennium, most central banks in the Western world have followed the same playbook. We will follow these developments up to the current situation at the time of writing this chapter, August 2022.

A new Conservative-led coalition took power in Norway in 2001. From December 2002 to March 2004, Norges Bank reduced its key interest rate from 7.0% to 1.75%. It is unclear whether it was once again the government that influenced the central bank to do so. In any case, it did not take steps that led to the central bank to stalling. The expansionary monetary policy was the start of a new period of high demand, and the consumption increased in Norway by 15% from 2005 to 2007.

New bubbles were inflated in the equity and housing markets. The real estate bubble burst in the US in 2007, before the securities bubble burst both in the US and in the rest of the world in 2008. This has since become known as *the Great Financial Crisis,* or simply the *Financial Crisis*. It can be traced back to the Federal Reserve's money printing after the crises that arose in 1987, 2000 and 2001.

The repeated central bank-led rescue operations sent a signal to the banks and the rest of the financial markets that they would bail all the major companies out of the problems that they suffered if they took too high a risk. The crash in 2008 was triggered by the collapse of the American investment bank Lehman Brothers. The bank had speculated on investment in so-called *garbage loans*, i.e., those loans that that US borrowers were most likely not able to repay. The bank had taken far too much risk. At the same time, many of the banks were borrowers and lenders to each other in a global, unfathomable, and infinitely large dichotomy of contracts that no one had a full overview of. No one knew which one of the other banks might have problems, the confidence in the market faded to black, and the supply of loans suddenly dried up. The system came to its knees because of a sudden lack of access to newly created money.

The financial crisis spread at lightspeed precipitating, again, a global stock market crash. Stock markets in Oslo and the New York fell by about 50%. In Norway, average house prices fell by 18% in two years, a fall that was about as rapid as the post-crash period of 1987. In the US, median house prices fell by about 23% over a two-year period.

In 2008, the Federal Reserve once again stepped in and bailed out the financial sector. This time, the central bank created several joint stock companies, called *the Maiden Lane companies*, which bought securities from banks that were in trouble. Whereas previously central banks only bought government bonds and similar securities from banks, the Maiden Lane companies began to buy all kinds of securities held by banks, including shares in large companies. These interventions caused the stock markets to rise, and the rescue operation was therefore viewed much in the same way as if they were aimed at the stock market as they were aimed at the banking system. Other central banks followed suit and distributed emergency money.

Banks did not immediately use all the money that central banks gave them in exchange for securities. Instead of lending all the money to citizens and businesses, they deposited much more money than they would normally do into central banks' reserve accounts, where the banks received a small profit from the interest.

Unlike the follow-up to the crash in 1987, Norges Bank in 2008 chose to lower the interest rate instead of raising it. After a Conservative-led coalition took over government power for the third time in about thirty years in 2013, Norges Bank reduced its key interest rate to such an extent that it was hovering just above zero for a long time. The other central banks followed suit. The consequence of which was that banks worldwide provided loans to customers at sub-zero interest when adjusted for growth in the consumer prices. This situation persists at the time of writing. Bank customers responded by taking out huge loans.

When the COVID-19 pandemic hit in 2020, states did three things:

(1) Lockdown of society, with cessation of production of goods and services

(2) Payment of huge amounts of economic support directly to many companies, so that they could continue to pay wages to their employees

(3) Increased the money supply enormously to allow governments to finance their expenditures

The combination of lockdown, low borrowing rates and the massive increase in access to money had the following consequences:

- People's bank account holdings grew
- Speculative investment in the housing market
- Speculative investment in the stock market

The S&P 500 index, which includes the 500 largest U.S. publicly traded companies, rose 68% from March 2020 to the end of the year, that is, in a year when the real economy was put on hold. The S&P/Case-Schiller US National Home Price Index rose by 43% from June 2020 to June 2022. We saw the same trends in the equity and housing markets in Norway. In simple terms, the governments stuffed their newly created money directly into the pockets of those in society that already were wealthy, at the same time as they led citizens and investors to speculate wildly in real estate.

**The stock market crash in the beginning of 2022**

In November 2021, the Federal Reserve announced that it would stop flooding the financial market with emergency money. The news affected some stocks negatively almost immediately, before the general stock market crash began for real in January 2022. The crash was compounded by Russia's invasion of Ukraine in February 2022.

In March, the Federal Reserve completely stopped the so-called *quantitative easing*. Over the previous two years, it had provided the economy with emergency money worth 4.6 trillion USD.

In June, the Federal Reserve had close to 9 trillion dollars' worth of paper assets on its balance sheet. The Federal Reserve reported that it aimed to sell securities at a book value of 3.3 trillion USD and in this way reduce the number of dollars in circulation. The NASDAQ technology index on the New York Stock Exchange had fallen nearly 50% at its peak. The Dow Jones index, an index with a traditionally broader composition of stocks in companies from several sectors, had fallen nearly 25% at its peak.

It was especially the share prices of large international entertainment and technology companies that fell the furthest. Since the beginning of 2022, Netflix's shares at the time of writing (July 25th, 2022) have fallen by 63% and Meta (Facebook) by 50%. This shows that *it is the digital economy that has experienced the biggest adjustment*. The sectors that fall the least will then be worth *relatively* more than the companies in the digital economy. This is a new but positive redistribution of resources that reverses the trend that took place while the money supply increased considerably, and speculation was at its worst.

The development in the Oslo Stock Exchange over the same period has not been as dramatic. By June 2022, it had fallen by 10%. However, what most of the mainstream media do not seem to grasp, was that the Norwegian krone depreciated considerably against the major currencies, at its peak 15 % against the US dollar. If you measure the stock market decline in dollars instead of kroner, the fall is comparable to the Dow Jones index, approx. 25%.

In July and August, yields on US 2-year treasuries have been higher than on 10-year treasuries, which in the past has been a key harbinger of an impending economic nosedive. According to Peter Warren's podcast *Tid er Penger* (Time is Money), it is reported that there is a prevalent trend in August 2022 that the big players are hedging their bets, while private investors have increasingly taken over as buyers. What's happening? It is likely that the financial elite are letting go of risky assets that the smaller players are hoovering up. At the same time, many hope that central banks will conjure more emergency money.

**Interest rate hikes and a housing market in limbo**

Central banks have begun to raise interest rates. The Federal Reserve's first interest rate hike in the summer of 2022 was 3/4 of a percentage point, while Norges Bank raised the interest rate by half percentage point. It is not a given that this will lead to a general decline in prices in the housing market, but increasingly it seems to be a likelihood.

**Fall in real estate market affects growth in money supply**

Both the financial sector and homeowners are eagerly tracking the fluxes and trends in the housing market. The financial sector is aware that the ability to get more money into the securities market will be negatively affected if property prices do not start rising again. A continued levelling off will mean that the multiplication effect that we looked at earlier ceases, which contributes to slower growth in the money supply.

If a fall in property values leads banks to demand more collateral and extraordinary repayment of loans, and borrowers are unable to meet the requirements, the multiplier effect may also be reversed. Then it may culminate in housing foreclosures and debt arrangements, forcing banks to write off receivables and thereby directly reducing the money supply. Such losses erode banks' equity capital, and at that point it won't take long before some of the banks are at risk of bankruptcy.

**Narrow exit**

If, for example, the prices of securities and property fall abruptly, "everyone" wants to sell. The process is not as fast as one might imagine with respect to the word "crash", which gives the dubious impression of suddenness. The exit is narrow, and there is not enough room for everyone who wants to get out at the same time at a price that they feel they can accept. It simply takes time to let the air out of the balloon. It is possible to burst it, but few have both the incentives and the financial muscles to do so.

**The function of countercyclical measures**

From a political perspective, it is logical to spend extra money during downturns, whether it is spending of tax revenues or financed by other means, as recommended by Keynes and the Oslo School. The reason is that it is popular in many groups, including:

- the working class, because the workers believe that this policy gives them safer workplaces
- politicians, because they get an economic argument for collecting more in taxes and fees, which allows them to spend money on something that increases their chances of re-election
- the construction industry, because states typically spend the money on large development projects
- economists, because they are given a central role in managing the projects, and in analyzing the interaction between state and private actors to assess profit opportunities in the financial industry
- the financial industry because countercyclical policy provides a safety net

The governments' use of citizens' tax money softens the landing when markets crash. It doesn't necessarily turn the markets around, but it gives the "smart money" more time to get others to take over the bad positions and the risks they possess.

**Other measures that aim at helping the big players**

If things start to look bleak for banks and large listed companies, the system has a variety of tools that can be activated to help them out of the crisis without causing them excessive losses:

- the stock exchange suspends trading if prices fall too abruptly

- the government allows banks to close extraordinarily to prevent customers from withdrawing their deposits
- the government issues guarantees to companies that find themselves in trouble, or bail out the companies' creditors and owners with direct buyouts, etc.

**Forcing down artificially high values**

In a declining market, some players want to "go short", otherwise known as “shorting the stock”, which means that they invest in financial instruments that make it possible to make a profit when the price of for instance the stocks of a publicly listed company fall. The investors who bet on lower stock prices are just as important for a well-functioning securities market as those who bet on prices going up. However, investors who try to speculate that the prices of equities are going down will need "deep pockets" and must be willing to take greater risks. They are also dependent on possessing a great deal of knowledge about securities markets and how exposed the players are for them to succeed. These investors can face several strong opponents:

- Large investors, such as so-called *hedge funds*, that have bet on a continued positive development in the stock market, and that risk huge losses if the true value of the stocks are exposed
- Banks. They primarily make money when the money supply increases. Therefore, they have incentives to place themselves on the other side of the bets, and make sure that prices do not fall
- Central banks. Without warning they can start printing new emergency money and buying up securities to prevent prices from falling

In the face of such opponents, speculators who go short risk losing their entire bet. On the other hand, profits may be enormous if they are successful. The more artificially high the value of something has become due to monetary inflation, the more there is to gain from it for those who succeed in forcing the price down to a more realistic level.

Richard Cantillon, who first assisted John Law in setting up his banking business, became the world's richest man when he placed his bet on a collapse of the Mississippi company in 1720. In 1992, investor George Soros managed to make a fortune by forcing Britain to devalue, that is to say, reduce the value of the Great British Pound (GBP). Soros attained legendary status in the financial community and was later called *The Man Who Broke the Bank of England.*

The current situation is that the value of real estate and securities has been so inflated over such a long period of time and in so many countries around the world, that enormous profit opportunities have presented themselves for those who dare to risk their money on the advent of another huge crash. Stock markets have already fallen a great deal in 2022, but market participants disagree on whether the worst is over or whether they should continue to fall. Central banks' monetary policy has probably been one of the most important factors in the last hundred years, and much depends on whether they resume their production of emergency money. Experience shows that if a new crisis arises, it takes a short time for them to fire up the printing press.

**Betting on hyperinflation**

One can also make a financial bet on hyperinflation. For example, you borrow as much as possible with a fixed interest rate agreement, and buy everything you can of physical assets, such as real estate, factories, silver, and gold. Inflation "eats up" your debt, and the sale of a small part of what you have bought can be used to pay it down. The German investor Hugo Stinnes grew enormously wealthy after he successfully speculated during hyperinflation in Germany in the 1920s.

**The business cycle – a summary**

In summary, large fluctuations from boom to bust can normally be explained by changes in growth in the money supply. There is no evidence that a large increase in the money supply has contributed to anything positive. The wild price fluctuations in the real estate and securities markets indicate that there has been an enormous redistribution of wealth, that we have had extremely costly restructuring phases and that the purchasing power of countries and citizens has been weakened. Former governor of Norges Bank, Svein Gjedrem, summarized his views on the effects of inflation in a presentation in 2004:

> History shows that higher growth cannot be achieved in exchange for higher inflation in the long run. An economic policy that fuels inflation does not generate higher economic growth. On the contrary, it lays the groundwork for later declines and unemployment.

This is one example that shows that the economists in the Austrian School's views on inflation are no longer controversial. However, mainstream economists seem to be no closer to proposing the abolition of the fiat monetary system.

**Cost of living after the financial crisis and the COVID-19 pandemic**

When central banks printed money, they bought securities from banks during the financial crisis in 2008, and many feared that consumer prices would skyrocket and in worst case that hyperinflation could occur. That didn't happen. There were probably two important reasons for this:

The first being that the banks refrained from lending all the money they had received. The second reason being that the crisis swore people off spending money. Instead, many chose to save their money, presumably because they wanted to wait to see how the economy fared.

As previously mentioned, in 2020, most states repealed banks' reserve requirements when the COVID-19 pandemic began to spread with gusto. Central banks additionally printed crisis money that governments distributed to businesses and the population. Money poured into society. Many continued to receive their pay-packets, but times were uncertain, and they saved more money than they would ordinarily have done. Running parallel to this, the production of goods and services ground to a halt. Towards the end of the pandemic, money began to burn a hole in people's pockets, and when states ended widespread restrictions, it became abundantly clear what happens when too many dollars "chase" too few goods and services. For prices, the only way was up, much to the chagrin of the consumer.

**What happened with the gold?**

As mentioned, Gresham's law says that bad money drives out good money. But now that the entire world economy is based on fiat money, where in the world did all the gold end up?

The gold that has been mined throughout history is still intact, spread around the world. According to *gold.org*, the best estimate is that 205,238 tons of gold have been mined.

Even though governments abandoned the gold standard, the central banks still own the most gold. According to figures from 2021, the U.S. holds more than 8,100 tons. That's roughly equivalent to the amount the next three on the list hold, Germany (3,300), Italy (2,500) and France (2,400), combined. Russia (2,300) is fifth and China (2,000) is sixth. In total, this is 10% of all the gold that has been mined.

These are only *reported figures*. The states may also hold gold that they do not report. On March 3rd, 2022, *moneyweek.com* published a piece in which Dominic Frisby reviewed China's own gold production and the purchase of foreign gold mining. He concluded that China has about 31 tons of gold, including 2.5 tons owned by private individuals safely housed in their jewelry boxes.

U.S. Global Investors wrote on its website in 2021 that central banks were previously net *sellers* of gold, but that as of 2010, they became net *buyers*. The US technology exchange NASDAQ wrote on its website in May 2022 that the largest gold buyers in the last ten years were Russia, Turkey, India, Poland and China.

New Zealand, Canada and Norway have reported offloading their gold reserves. Norges Bank sold theirs in 2004. Their website states that:

> [It] has sold its gold reserves apart from seven gold bars for exhibition purposes and 3 1/2 tons of gold coins that were part of the "gold transport" to England at the outbreak of war in 1940. Norges Bank no longer uses gold as part of its international reserves.

This means that Norges Bank has sold almost all the gold that Norwegian civilians and soldiers narrowly failed to salvage when Germany invaded Norway. The value of the 46.5 tons of gold from the gold transport sold by Norges Bank is approximately 28 billion NOK.

One might wonder why the largest central banks have continued to stockpile gold. What interest do they have in holding gold when they no longer are operating with a gold standard? One may also ask why the three central banks mentioned above sold their gold. Moreover, it is tempting to ask whether these are bank-led self-assessments, or whether any of them decided how much gold to buy and sell on the basis of agreements with other central banks. It would not come as a surprise if it were the Federal Reserve that has asked Norges Bank to sell off its gold reserves.

As always when looking at **the big picture**, it's more important to explore what an actor in this crucible is actually doing than to speculate or second guess as to the motives and what truly lies beneath. It is important to note that the largest and most powerful central banks still own a lot of gold and some of them continue in their acquisition of it. They have great power when it comes to shaping future economic policy, and what they *do* is a more accurate sign of what will happen in the future than what they *say*.

There is some publicly available information about privately owned companies that own a lot of gold, and it shows that they do not own anywhere near as much as the central banks. However, knowing how much gold the wealthiest buy, is very difficult to say with any measure of certainty. In 2018, Global Bullion Suppliers published an article stating that the entire population of India owns about 24,000 tons of gold, mostly as jewelry. This accounts for 12% of all of the gold that has ever been mined.

Who knows – if the current fiat money system collapses, Indian citizens might find themselves clambering up the list of the richest people in the world. The question is whether citizens and businesses in other countries should follow the example of the citizens of India.

# Today's situation

**Introduction**
In this chapter, we look at where the inflation economy has shifted scarce resources, i.e., which sectors have attracted the value of real estate, labor and capital, and who controls them.

**Global wealth**
According to the Boston Consulting Group, the world economy's financial wealth and real asset pool grew by 10.6% in 2021, to almost 530 trillion USD.

The International Monetary Fund (*IMF*) has predicted that it will grow by 3.2% in 2022.

**Global growth in debt and money supply**
We have seen that most of the money is created when banks enter loan agreements. Growth in the money supply will therefore largely follow the growth in debt.

According to the IMF, global debt grew by 28% in 2020 and ended at 226 trillion USD at the end of the year.

According to the *Institute of International Finance*, it grew by 33% in 2021.

In total, *global debt growth was 70% in a two-year period.*

At the end of 2021, the world's total debt was more than 300 trillion USD.

**The Americans' debt**
US government debt amounts to 30 trillion USD, US households are 16 trillion USD in debt, and non-financial corporations are 12 trillion USD in debt, i.e., a total of 58 trillion USD.

Excluding the financial sector, Americans are the debtors of nearly 20% of the 300 trillion USD of credit-generated money in circulation in the world.

**Who owns the US national debt**
The Federal Reserve owns 25% of U.S. government debt, while foreign investors own two-thirds.

Japanese investors own the largest share of Americans' foreign debt, 1.3 trillion USD as of May 2022. Japan itself has the equivalent of 12 trillion USD in government debt, which is the highest per capita in the world. It is likely that Japan's stake in the US government debt is as a direct result of the Japanese central bank's enormous money printing in recent years. This is an example of government borrowing in the US being financed not only by the Federal Reserve's money printing, but also by other central banks' money printing activities.

China is the US governments second largest creditor, while the UK ranks third.

**The status of the dollar as the world reserve currency**
The dollar's share of the world's bank reserves has fallen from 85% in the early 1970s to 70% around year 2000, and to 60% in 2022. The development of this has not been linear.

The dollar is used in 40% of global trade, while the US share of this trade accounts for only 10%.

The Euro is the second largest currency, ahead of the British Pound, Japanese Yen and Chinese Yuan.

**Government growth**
In the US, the federal government's share of GDP has risen from 7% in 1902 to 21% after World War II, before rising further to 41% during the financial crisis in 2008 and 45% in 2020.

According to Statistics Norway's article from 1965, *The Norwegian economy after the war*, the public sector's share of GDP went from 6% in 1900 to 31% in 1962. If we jump ahead to 2020, according to OECD surveys, this figure was 66%.

**The share of the financial industry**
The financial industry, including insurance accounts for 9% of GDP in the US and 7% in Norway.

**The share of the non-profit sector**
The non-profit sector accounts for about 6% of GDP in the U.S. and 4% in Norway.

**The rest of the GDP**
It is the "rest of" GDP that will be responsible for the production of goods and services that the government, the financial industry and the non-profit sector cannot produce. If we subtract the share of government, financial sectors and non-profit enterprises, this residual share of GDP amounts to only 40% in the US and 23% in Norway.

**Agriculture**
After World War II, agriculture's share of GDP in Norway was 7%, while it is now only 0.5%. That has a parity with the U.S., where agriculture currently accounts for 0.6% of GDP.

After global prices for agricultural produce came to a standstill between 1975 and 2005, they have risen in recent years. But so indeed have farmers' costs, which in

Norway led to the closure of 17.4% of all agricultural holdings in the period 2010 to 2020.

**Energy and food crisis**
The energy and food prices have been rising dramatically all over the world, and in September 2022, the World Food Programme, itself a part of the UN system, warned that we are threatened by a global food crisis. A combination of climate policies, environmental policies and the war in Ukraine affect supply adversely.

**The digital economy**
According to the World Bank, the digital economy is growing two and a half times as fast as the rest of the economy. In 2022, it accounts for more than 15% of global value added.

**Health services**
Increasingly health services have become something that politicians believe should either be provided by the public sector or mandated by governmental regulation, and the general trend is that health workers occupy an increasingly larger share of the total workforce. In Norway this has tipped over into the extreme, as 1 out of 5 workers are employed in the health services sector. In the Netherlands it is a 1 out of 6 ratio, in USA is 1/7, Canada 1/9, Austria 1/10, Italy 1/13 and Russia 1/16.

The pivotal point here is that the more health services you get, the longer you live, and the more health services you need. When somebody else than the patient pays for the service, it is almost guaranteed to spiral out of control, as we now see happening in Norway. Here it is expected that the ratio will increase to 1 out of 3. It is akin to the phenomena "the tragedy of the commons", so called by economists, whereby there is overconsumption of a free economic resource, such as fish in a lake, until none remain.

**Economic inequality in the US**
During the COVID-19 pandemic, the wealth of the so-called *'one-percenters'* in the United States increased by more than 33%.

At the end of 2021, the one-percenters owned 32.3% of Americans' assets.

The richest 10% owned 70%, up from 61% in 1989.

The lower 50% owned a total of 2.5%.

The share of middle-class households fell from 61% in 1970 to 50% in 2021. The middle class's share of society's total income fell over the same period by one-third, from 62 to 42%.

**One-percenters in Norway**
Norway is one of the countries with the least economic inequality in the world, but the difference is growing, and now the one-percenters own more than 20% of Norwegians' assets.

**One-percenters worldwide**
The one-percent richest people in the world own half of the global wealth. This could hint that the one-percenters in the US and Norway are imbued of quite positive growth prospects.

According to Forbes, the number of dollar billionaires in the world in 2021 increased by 32% from 2,095 to a record 2,755.

**Europe**
The OECD reports that real growth in Europe's six largest economies has declined continuously since the 1990s, and that there has been almost zero growth in Europe's overall economy over the past twenty years. In short, Europe is becoming a statistical and literal irrelevance with respect to the development of the world economy. Europeans stand idle and watch as growth flourishes in the East and the richest Americans grow richer still.

**The households' financial situation**
According to Norges Bank, households in Norway have more debt today than they had before the crash in 1987. At the end of 2021, the average in Norway was 2.46 times disposable income, almost as much as Denmark, which is the "world leader" in these statistics, while the average in the US was 1.01, according to the OECD. The figure for the US should be seen through the prism which reveals that 65% of the American households own their own homes (compared to 80% in Norway), that credit card debt rose by 17% from August 2021 to August 2022, and that 17% of the households are no longer able to pay their electricity bills. At the same time, UK media reports that the general population are struggling to pay their bills. Indeed, as of the time of writing, the darkly foreboding phrase "to eat or heat" has entered day-to-day lexicon in the UK.

**Real estate**
Media outlets reported on September 8th, 2022, that apartment prices in the Swedish capital Stockholm had fallen by 11% in only 3 months. In comparison, the prices of villas across the country had fallen only by 4% in the same period. On September 11th house prices were discovered to be falling in 98 of the 148 major housing markets in the US. In 11 markets that figure was 5%. The biggest corrections were found in areas dominated by big tech, San Francisco and San Jose, which were down 8.2% from its 2022 peak, and Seattle, down 7.8%. House prices in Auckland, New Zealand, fell 18 % from November 2021 to July 2022, while prices

levelled off in Norway over summer 2022, before they again began climbing in August.

**Summary**

**The big picture** is as follows:

- We have witnessed the largest money-printing experiment in history, and currently fiat money equivalent to $300 trillion in credit-created money chases $530 trillion worth of assets
- It is likely that a combination of lockdown, money printing on an industrial scale and debt growth made the super-rich even richer
- Money printing and borrowing are the main tools in the struggle for control of the world's wealth
- Both governments and one-percenters seem content to let the other party grow
- The dollar's status as the world's reserve currency is declining
- Households are probably not able to withstand a serious economic downturn
- Many see the value of their homes falling at record speed

We should also take note of the following:

- Debt must continue to grow if there is to be enough money available in the world to pay interest on the loans. The 70% increase in debt that we saw in the last two years indicates that we will see further debt growth in the years to come. It also indicates that interest rates cannot be raised substantially, because credit growth then slows, resulting in less access to money that can be used to pay interest. It is likely that debt growth will far exceed economic growth. It is also likely that growth in the money supply will leady many countries to struggle with hyperinflation
- The sectors that respond most rapidly to the inflation economy (the state, the financial sector and the digital economy) attract huge shares of the available real estate, labor and capital. As a result, there is little left for the real economy to produce goods and services for the citizens and the business sector
- The simple explanation for the food crisis is that everything that grows in the inflation economy pulls resources away from agriculture, while population growth continues. In Norway, the problems are compounded by the fact that the agricultural sector is completely dominated by planned economic policies. The same is largely true in the EU
- The digital economy is probably *the great speculation bubble* of our time. The rapid growth in this sector is at the expense of the rest of the

economy and is likely to weaken both productivity and the real economy's ability to meet people's needs

- The extremely high share of workers employed in the health services might be the greatest *politically managed bubble* of our time, at least in Norway
- The negative trend for the American middle class indicates that American society today bears a greater share of the problems of the inflation economy itself. This may be related to the decline in the dollar's position as a reserve currency

# Channelization

As we have seen, it is a general feature that money inflation leads to a large degree of *channelization in the economy*. This is particularly due to newly printed fiat money outcompeting money created via work, and that the new fiat money thus attracts real estate, labor and capital as if they are powerful magnets.

The newly created money first flows into the securities market and the real estate market. This means, among other things, that we do not experience a similar rise in prices for everything, and that inflation therefore distributes advantages and disadvantages unequally in society.

The growth in the government and the financial industry is as a result of monetary inflation being channeled to the government via loans, taxes, and excise duties, while it is channeled to the real economy via financial markets.

Commodity prices are rising the least of all assets because they are far out in the chain of transactions with newly created money.

The money is channeled into the central areas, instead of spreading throughout the countryside. This pulls labor and capital away from the outskirts, including from the agricultural sector.

With respect to the more situation-based channels of money inflation, we see that the US strategy was to ensure that the world commodity market would be traded in dollars, following the agreement with Saudi Arabia on petrodollars against weapons. We also saw that in the period following the financial crisis in 2008, banks channeled emergency money to their reserve accounts towards the central banks.

New fiat money is channeled in the direction of markets characterized by speculation. The bigger the influx of new money, the greater the risk recipients need to take if they want to preserve the purchasing power of that money. This precipitates more and more speculation. As prices begin to rise and the story of all the newly rich begins to reveal themselves, the rest of society loses ground, and more people are drawn into the game. In 1637 money found its way to the tulip market in the Netherlands, in 1720 it was the Mississippi Company in France, in 1929 the stock exchanges, especially in London and New York, in the 1980s it was both the real estate market and the stock exchanges, after 2000 it was again the real estate market and stock exchanges, especially the digital economy. As of 2020, there has been a gigantic influx of speculative money into the cryptocurrency market.

Gresham's law ensures that silver and gold are channeled out of countries with unhealthy monetary policies, and into countries that accept all kinds of money. Afterwards, capital and labor find the same path. The countries that want to make the most of the fiat money take all kinds of measures against gold, both by seizing it and by prohibiting the purchase and export of it. Inflation policy by definition enshrines a war against gold that leads to gold possessing an artificially low value.

Furthermore, we have seen that hyperinflation channels fiat money out of the economy, while silver and gold return. It logically follows, then, that the value of silver and gold rises more than any other economic goods, as there is a need for a universally recognized exchange medium.

# Political initiatives and the media

The thing that characterizes discussions taking place about inflation today is that there is almost no one to address the fact that inflation is a policy, that it is an increase in the money supply leading to an enormous redistribution of wealth.

In August 2022 US president Joe Biden launched a proposal for a law called *The Inflation Reduction Act*. The law has not been passed at the time of writing. The proposal calls for the authorities to take a larger share of the costs of prescription medicines and the transition to climate-friendly energy. In addition, it includes funding for almost 87,000 new tax agents, i.e., new hires in the Internal Revenue Service (the IRS). In presenting the proposal, Biden claims that the law will lead to hundreds of billions of dollars in budget deficit reductions. It means that the Biden administration will continue its policy of budget deficits, which traditionally involve expanding the money supply. Most economists commenting on this in the media seem to question how this law can reduce inflation.

In Norway now, it is electricity that worries politicians. They have so far solved galloping prices in a good old planned economic spirit by giving money to private customers, that is, a kind of *electricity social benefit scheme*. The EU has taken it a step further, as they seek to introduce price caps on natural gas.

At the national level in the United States and Norway there is no debate in the media or among politicians about the inflation system upon which our society is based. This is likely because very few politicians and media people know much about inflation and its origins.

The BRICS countries, Brazil, Russia, India, China and South Africa, have been working for some time to introduce a new common currency that can replace the dollar as the world's reserve currency. They occasionally provide some statements about this, but it garners scant media attention in the West.

There are quite a few people in the cryptocurrency community who discuss the fiat money system. There are also several economists who have started to get involved. However, this is again something that the mainstream media cares little about.

To conclude, politicians have little regard for the fiat money system as a political issue, and the mainstream media the same. This means that it is the people who must get involved if we are to elevate it on the politicians' agenda.

# Discussion

**Introduction**

In this chapter, we use what we have learned in the previous chapters to discuss some of the most important issues related to inflation, including:

- Whether inflation is good for the economy
- If the system really is based on trust
- The alternative to inflation policy

**Is inflation good?**

Several economists have argued that inflation is good, because it *'greases the gears of the economy'*. However, they have not been able to present a convincing argument based on logical deduction, neither on the basis of any empirical analysis. Inflation is a policy, and nothing more. It is based on a silent consensus between the two most powerful groups in society, the two groups that at the same time benefit the most: the state and the financial sector. This is a truly dangerous political equilibrium.

As we have seen, history shows that inflation is about a good many things that include: a breach of promise; fraud; redistribution of wealth; the build-up of state power; gifts to the financial elite; centralization; depopulation of rural areas; power struggles; the boom-and-bust cycle; speculation; destruction of savings; debt growth; financing of military forces and warfare. In my opinion there is nothing good about inflation. The fact that some groups benefit from inflation is not in total a valid enough argument.

On the contrary – inflation is societally destructive. The most terrifying aspect is that inflation simultaneously destroys society while creating an illusion of economic progress. As I see it, inflation is simply the perfect fraud, while also the largest fraud.

Nation States' systematic use of inflation as a policy began to plague Europe almost 2,500 years ago, when Athens introduced it to finance the war against Sparta. It has plagued Trøndelag and the rest of Norway for almost 1,000 years since Harald Hardråde killed Einar Tambarskjelve and his son Eindride and set up the mints in Hamar and Nidaros in 1050. It has been akin to a global plague for 100 years since the representatives of the Bank of England and the Federal Reserve conspired against the rest of the world when they worked together to introduce the first gold exchange standard in the 1920s.

Since the early 20th century, the majority of economists have argued that a little inflation is good for the economy. Considering that the field of economics has embraced empirical studies as a method during this period, it is curious that they have not yet presented data showing that this is in fact correct. Surely, the miserable and miserly economic development that we have experienced in recent decades in western countries indicates that inflation has had the opposite effect. Nor can the postulate be proven through logical deduction. Contrarily, economists of the Austrian School show that inflation must necessarily lead to overinvestment, malinvestment, uneconomical use of resources, speculation, and large market fluctuations.

The postulate that inflation is good for the economy, was the financial Cassandra politicians needed to put in place a global inflation policy in order to enrich themselves at everyone else's expense. In my view, this is the most dangerous theory that has ever to escape from academia. It is so dangerous that most of the Universities in Norway, the US and all other countries presumably find the prospect of dealing with it extremely daunting. Instead, they continue to look in the other direction.

**Economic illiteracy**

It is a tragedy that only an infinitesimal percentage of the population understands something as important as the true nature of money alongside the connection between the control of the money supply and inflation by states and the financial elite. It represents an opportunity for the few who understand the system to perversely exploit it at the expense of everyone else. In fact, this is precisely what has happened. As John Maynard Keynes told us in the book that he wrote in 1919, *The Economic Consequences of the Peace*:

> By this means the government may secretly and unobserved, confiscate the wealth of the people, and not one man in a million will detect the theft.

The reason for the situation remaining the same today, is as a result of governments and economists forcing everybody to stare myopically at the prices, instead of focusing on how the expansion of the money supply redistributes scarce economic resources.

If all pupils and students had been taught the history of economics including how money is *actually* created, we may have quite conceivably avoided the situation we find ourselves mired in today. The way I see it, it is a fundamental human right for new generations to be educated about the ways in which governments have systematically used inflation as a means of deceiving its people. Additionally, a lesson on the close relationship between inflation and war is in order. It should be the duty of all schools to include this in their respective curriculums.

**Is the system based on trust?**

Is it correct, as many argue, that "today's monetary system is based solely on trust"?

In my opinion, the answer to this is a resolute and deafening NO. That argument is based on two fundamental assumptions: that we are free to choose; and that we have a basic understanding of how the monetary system works. However, this is not the case at all. Instead, the system rests on two pillars:

- Coercion, because people are forced to pay taxes with the state's fiat money, which gives the fiat money an artificial high value
- Delusion, because people mistakenly focus on price stability instead of the redistributive effects of money production

What we really trust is that the value of our fiat money will continue to depreciate. If we were allowed to choose freely, we would see the true meaning of the word trust. Then we would use money that remained stable in value or that became more valuable over time.

**The fear of deflation**

A recurring argument against stabilizing the money supply or pegging the currency to the value of gold, is that deflation, i.e., that money becomes more valuable over time, is dangerous. Politicians and central banks claim that people and businesses will hoard money if they believe that it will be worth more, that they will stop consuming and that they will not invest, that businesses will go bankrupt, unemployment will rise and that the result will be a recession.

We'll first take a look at the empirical basis for that claim. In a 2004 article entitled *Deflation and Depression: Is There an Empirical Link?* economists Andrew Atkeson and Patrick Kehoe at the Federal Reserve Bank of Minneapolis write:

> *... the only episode in which we find evidence of a link between deflation and depression is the Great Depression (1929-34). We find virtually no evidence of such a link in any other period. ... What is striking is that nearly 90% of the episodes with deflation did not have depression. In a broad historical context, beyond the Great Depression, the notion that deflation and depression are linked virtually disappears.*

This indicates that it would be difficult to find empirical evidence that proves that deflation causes economic downturns. The deflationary period and depression in the United States after the stock market crash of 1929 was as a result of, as we have previously seen, Hoover not allowing the largest speculation bubbles in world history to burst, choosing instead to solve the problems with planned economic measures thereby exacerbating the situation. In other words, the recession had nothing to do with a stable money supply or gold.

Economists also use what happened in the 1920s in many European countries as an argument that deflation is dangerous. In all likelihood this is because economic history has been given low priority in the education of economists. The deflation of the 1920 was politically created and was not caused by the gold standard. In Europe, variations in the value of money from the time the war broke out in 1914 and through the 1920s were solely due to monetary policy. Central banks first printed money at an enormous pace and government borrowing was completely out of control, causing the money supply to multiply. Subsequently, they began to drastically reduce the money supply over a short period of time.

With reference to the argument that people will stop consuming, we can assume that users are roughly divided into two groups: the first group does not have the opportunity to stop consuming, because they live on a subsistence minimum of income. In the second group, the big picture today is that many take out loans instead of saving. Many do so because they expect inflation to "eat up" what they owe to the bank. Others borrow because their neighbor is borrowing.

It's the same with investments. Today, investment is to a large extent financed by borrowing, and the reasons are broadly the same as debt-financed consumption.

With deflation, this is turned on its head. People who do not live at a subsistence minimum will then save more. This means that they will adjust both their consumption and their investments so that it stands in a reasonable proportion to how much they have saved. Over time, consumption and investment will to a greater extent be based on savings and current income rather than loans. As people save money, they will lend their savings to others who want to invest, or they invest their savings as equity in companies. Sustainable consumption and investment require healthy savings.

Anyone who continues to claim that deflation is caused by monetary freedom , or that money is linked to gold is harmful, has a major task ahead of them.

**Emergency money for banks**

Emergency money sends the wrong signals to banks and the rest of society. Banks retain their profits when the economy is doing well, while the risk of large losses is reduced significantly as the central bank provides them with a safety net such as this. A direct consequence is that banks take on much higher risk than they would normally have done if the central bank allowed them to enter into bankruptcy. The higher the risk, the higher the chance of collapse.

The underlying rationale for saving the banks from bankruptcy is a postulate that a collapse of the *financial sector* would be devastating to *the real economy*. This is a statement worthy of a hostage-taking terrorist, ignoring that it is the financial sector that has grown out of the real economy, and not the other way around. If banks are not allowed to enter bankruptcy, they will take ever-greater risks, lay claim to more of society's scarce resources and ultimately destroy the real economy.

**Implications for security policy**

We have seen that inflation and war are easy bedfellows. The question is what the implications of present-day inflation policy on security policy are.

As the US has become increasingly indebted, an ever-greater interdependence has developed between the US as a military superpower and countries that themselves have inadequate military defenses, such as Norway and most other European countries. From the US government's perspective, the US risks that the dollar will become less in-demand among other countries leading the US to experience enormous financial problems and opening up the possibility that the US no longer wants or can protect the other countries militarily.

As Western countries have developed more decadent habits and prioritized entertainment and speculation, the BRICS countries, Brazil, Russia, India, China and South Africa, have also taken a larger share of the production of goods and services on which we actually depend. Russia's oil and gas deliveries are an example. Germany mothballed its coal-fired power plants and nuclear plants. The U.S. was supposed to slow down land-based oil extraction. Norway wanted to stop investing in oil exploration. Social engineers were supposed to lead us merrily into a green economic utopia, without considering the costs, without looking at the security policy consequences, and without first making sure to cure us of our dependence on fossil fuels. At the same time, the Western world shook their fingers disapprovingly at the countries that continued to extract and use a lot of coal, oil and gas, even though we were completely dependent on them increasing the rate of extraction if we ourselves were to scale back. Western leaders did not realize this until Russia invaded Ukraine in February 2022 and subsequently cut off gas supplies to Germany as retaliation when foreign governments froze Russian assets.

The US has chosen to view the growth of the BRICS countries as a competition that in the long term may pose a security policy threat. To the BRICS countries, U.S. rhetoric may seem like the Americans are considering using force against them instead of cleaning up their own economic mess. This further contributes to the build-up of foreign policy tension.

Russia's invasion of Ukraine can be interpreted politically as a *de facto* question to the Western countries as to whether they can afford to continue with the same policy. The reaction of the Western countries has been to redirect resources to the rearmament of their military forces. The problem for the West is how to finance the rearmament this time. As we have seen, inflation has been the usual way of doing things. For the West, however, the potential for inflation is likely to be exhausted at this stage. We are already at risk of hyperinflation because of all the influxes of new money. Should politicians possibly raise taxes instead?

It's as if the central bank governors in the Western world have poured paint on the floor, and now politicians are huddled in a corner, fumbling helplessly with their brushes.

Putin understood all of this long ago, and he talked about this in his speech on *St. Petersburg's International Economic Forum* on June 17, 2022. Among other things, he said:

> Surging inflation in product and commodity markets had become a fact of life long before the events of this year. The world has been driven into this situation, little by little, by many years of irresponsible macroeconomic policies pursued by the G7 countries, including uncontrolled emission and accumulation of unsecured debt. These processes intensified with the onset of the coronavirus pandemic in 2020, when supply and demand for goods and services drastically fell on a global scale...
>
> Because they could not or would not devise any other recipes, the governments of the leading Western economies simply accelerated their money-printing machines. Such a simple way to make up for unprecedented budget deficits...
>
> I have already cited this figure: over the past two years, the money supply in the United States has grown by more than 38%. Previously, a similar rise took decades, but now it grew by 38% or 5.9 trillion dollars in two years. By comparison, only a few countries have a bigger gross domestic product. The EU's money supply has also increased dramatically over this period. It grew by about 20%, or 2.5 trillion euros.
>
> Lately, I have been hearing more and more about the so-called – please excuse me, I really would not like to do this here, even mention my own name in this regard, but I cannot help it – we all hear about the so-called 'Putin inflation' in the West. When I see this, I wonder who they expect would buy this nonsense – people who cannot read or write, maybe.

> Anyone literate enough to read would understand what is actually happening.
>
> "The rising prices, accelerating inflation, shortages of food and fuel, petrol, and problems in the energy sector are the result of system-wide errors the current US administration and European bureaucracy have made in their economic policies. That is where the reasons are, and only there.

Putin, incidentally, "forgot" to mention that Russia increased its own money supply M2 by about 30% during the same period, that is, more than the euro bureaucracy that he criticized. I suspect that Russia would probably prefer to get other countries to accept fiat money that the Kremlin controls, rather than for the world to have a new and healthier monetary system.

However, what Putin pointed out here, was that people must be blind if they are going to buy the story that it is the war in Ukraine that is causing inflation. He seems unaware of how indoctrinated we are in the Western world when it comes to the promise that inflation is good, that children and young people are taught nothing of the sort in their time at school, and that our students are taught that the *money illusion* is beneficial for society.

**The Achilles' heel of a reserve currency**

The advantage that a government has when it controls a global reserve currency is that it can use inflation as a policy tool to grow without increasing taxes. All that remains is for the government to print new money and to run on debt-financed budget deficits, as the US has done for the better part of the previous 100 years.

If a small state attempts something that poses a threat to a currency's reserve status, the dominant state can use military or economic sanctions to prevent open rebellion.

The reserve status, however, has an Achilles' heel. Increased trade in oil and gas in a currency other than the dollar is one example. In 2014, Russia and China signed an agreement that China would buy large quantities of gas from Russia. The Western world's embargo on Russia after the invasion of Ukraine has also led to Russia selling more oil to Asian countries instead of the oil being traded in the global market. These transactions are not settled in dollars. This reduces oil and gas as a price inflation buffer for the dollar.

The reserve currency status will also suffer if one of the larger countries, such as China, scraps its fiat money and ties its yuan to gold. If that happens, capital is likely to quickly flow to China, as happened after the revolution in the Netherlands. While a transition from dollar-based trading in oil and gas to the use of another currency will most likely be a gradual process that will take many years, perhaps decades, to resolve. Thusly, a decision in China to link the currency to gold could have major consequences on a shorter timeline. We saw that it took only two years from Nixon appeared in the TV screen in 1971 until the dollar's association with gold disappeared completely in 1973. It probably takes longer for a government that does not have the reserve currency to completely change its monetary policy. China would prefer to have several other countries involved in doing the same before doing something this drastic, and this is therefore one of the topics discussed by the BRICS countries.

The dollar's position will also weaken if the other countries' central banks reduce their dollar reserves. They may also start buying more gold, as we see several of the major central banks have done over the past ten years. In this way, they make themselves less vulnerable if the value of the dollar depreciates. We can expect that this will lead the US putting pressure on other countries to *sell* gold instead. The question is how long such a strategy can be effective. When the West sees Russia and China increasing their gold reserves, more central banks will feel compelled to do the same. The other western countries can also point out that the US has more gold than anyone else, and question why they should not also have the right to have the same security. If households and enterprises start buying more gold, this could have the same effect.

If the dollar loses its reserve status, it means that fewer people will accept it in regular trading. However, it does not reduce the number of dollars in circulation. Whoever wants to spend their dollars must then send them to a place where they are accepted. Those dollars will typically be circulated back to the United States, where the government requires payment of taxes and fees in dollars. When "the chickens come home to roost" there will be an abundance of dollars chasing U.S. goods and services domestically, potentially with hyperinflation a resultant fact.

For naïve monetary policy underlings such as Norway and most other Western countries, the risk lies primarily in choosing to lash oneself to the mast and stand together with the Americans even though the days of the dollar as the worlds reserve currency are seemingly numbered. If so, there is a high probability that Norway will experience hyperinflation as well. If politicians think a little about their own nation's interests, they can make choices that reduce the risk of economic disaster. However, it is a prerequisite that they *actually understand* what inflation is and that it is indeed a policy.

**Cryptocurrencies**

Before I go on with a short discussion around this topic, please allow me to humbly proffer the following:

Firstly, it is not overstating it to consider how valuable the advent of the Bitcoin movement is to society's evolution of thought with respect to real-world economics. This development has educated so many people and wrested the discussions about fiat money and inflation out of the hands of a small elite of economists and governments.

Secondly, all efforts that go into facilitating safe storage of value and voluntary economic transactions outside a fiat monetary system that is abused by the states and the financial elite, should be applauded.

However, it is easy to be led by your heart rather than your head and think that the cryptocurrencies are a kind of threat to fiat money, and that the governments therefore prefer to get rid of them as competitors. When we think more carefully about this, that explanation does not seem that obvious. For instance, why have governments not long since banned the use of private cryptocurrency?

One reason may be that it will be expensive for states to use coercion to get rid of competition. Another reason may be that the competitiveness of national currency is sufficiently safeguarded by the fact that it must be used to pay taxes and duties. Such privileges therefore continue to give it an artificially high value.

By extension, the states may see the cryptocurrencies as beneficial to them. For the states, it is the redistributive effect of fiat money that is important, not the monetary monopoly itself. From that point of view, it makes good sense to say that the states instead see themselves benefitting from cryptocurrency's success. If speculation based on new money inflates the price of cryptocurrencies, the price of goods, services, shares in stocks and other securities will inflate to a lesser extent. This, in turn, gives states greater leeway to expand their money supply. That is, states may think that the more cryptocurrencies that are invented the better, because it increases the capacity of cryptocurrency as a price inflation buffer, while at the same time making it more difficult for a single cryptocurrency to compete with the state's fiat money.

The US has been able to export its inflation to other countries via, for example, the quasi gold standard, the oil market and eventually also the market for climate quotas. In addition, they can export some of the inflation to a cryptocurrency market that in November 2021 absorbed fiat money worth 3 trillion USD, that is, one trillion more than the global revenues from the sale of oil and gas. It is an irony of fate that many people who invest in cryptocurrency believe that this is some sort of rebellion against fiat money, while at the same time facilitates printing of more fiat money in practice.

The problem is that there is a risk that cryptocurrency bubbles will only delay the rise in prices for other goods and services, as was the case with the emergency money that banks chose to store in their central bank reserve accounts after the financial crisis in 2008. When a bubble bursts and everyone wants to cash out, those who are able to convert cryptocurrency into fiat money will have to place it in something else. The greater the capital flight, the greater the chance that the prices of goods and services that people actually need will go up.

The challenge for those who own cryptocurrencies is that the governments can one day create measures that leave them worthless. One thing is prohibition, but it doesn't take much regulation for them to be handicapped too much for them to function as money. If a government one day allows people to use whatever money they want or the states set up some sort of gold standard, it will also likely spell the end for most of them.

On January 17th, 2022, e24.no wrote that the tax authorities in Norway would intensify its control of those who had invested in cryptocurrency, after only approx. 1 in 20 of those that the authorities considered to have bought cryptocurrencies had declared it on their tax return. If you look at it in the context of the enormous boom in the cryptocurrency market during the pandemic, there is good reason to assume that Biden has the priorities ready for the almost 87,000 new tax agents that his Inflation Reduction Act is supposed to finance.

**Can inflation be controlled?**

If you have read this far it may have dawned on most of you that creating more money is one of the most powerful policies that exists in a society. The influx of new money makes a few rich and many poor, while the broad layer of the people are drawn into speculation in real estate, securities, and all manner of spurious capital.

We have also seen that control of the money went to the heads of both Harald Hardråde and Karl XII, and that this led them to take too much risk. We cannot exclude the possibility that inflation also leads to hubris among today's leaders within government and the financial industry, and that it is inflation that controls them, and not the other way around.

The Weimar Republic’s collapse has also taught us that hyperinflation transforms modern society into a gigantic primeval prison. It transforms people from perfectly decent human beings who largely trust each other to barbarians who employ hate, envy and deception as workaday tools when dealing with their neighbors.

The answer is clear, inflation is difficult to control, and the manifestly awful effects of hyperinflation are impossible to control.

**Unintended consequences of deliberate actions**

In other words, we have a dangerous situation in which nobody really benefits. In my view, this is a typical example of unintended consequences by way of deliberate actions. This is caused by the fact that influential academics, people from the financial elite and politicians have been given far too much latitude in order to leverage their own advantages with inflation as a policy. Quick profits have been shared by the few, while long-lasting effects are terribly negative and end up being carried by almost everyone.

**Capitalism will get the blame**

If the current monetary system collapses, politicians, the media, and many others are likely to blame capitalism. There will always be a specific person or company that steals the limelight, as it was with Johan Palmstruch, Georg Heinrich von Görtz, John Law and Lehman Brothers. This way, they will try to draw attention away from the fact that it is the governments that hold the primary responsibility for destroying our money. When, for example, the public sector in Norway spends two thirds of GDP, and the private sector must deal with a long list of state interventions, such as national and European regulation, taxes, and a steady expansion of the money supply, then blaming capitalism is an absurdity. We would be wise to remind ourselves that it was such accusations and misconceptions that in the 1920s and 1930s formed the basis for the inflation policy that we have today.

**The alternative to inflation policy: Monetary freedom**

James Turk, author of *Money and Liberty*, has said that nature supplies man with everything we need to make progress, including money. What he means is that valuable metals such as silver and gold have been recognized as money in society for thousands of years. This seems reasonable. There have only been a few brief periods since people were civilized that money has not found its roots in real values in some way. The period of the last century of quasi gold standards, and the last 50 years of a global one hundred percent pure fiat monetary system, only constitutes a minor part of world history. With that as a starting point, it seems more likely that the current system will soon be replaced by money that has some link to real, economic value.

In my view there is reason to believe that all governments that install a gold standard, will end up deceiving their citizens, as governments have done many times previously. Therefore, reestablishing monetary freedom is the only option. Here I define monetary freedom as *decentralized money*, where citizens freely decide which money they want to use and without any government regulation that gives a certain type of medium of exchange a privileged status. People would then get to use the money that they preferred. This was the case, for example, in the Viking Age in Norway before Harald Hardråde, and in the Netherlands in the 16th and the 17th century, and this is how we could have it today.

One may argue that it is impractical to reintroduce monetary freedom, for instance that it will be difficult for the government to collect taxes if we abolish the requirement to pay taxes with a specific type of money or currency. In my opinion it is not a bad thing if governments must reform and simplify their tax systems. Neither is it a bad thing if monetary freedom reduces governments' revenues. Simply put, the inflation economy has made the majority of them morbidly *obese*, and politicians and citizens are increasingly beginning to voice their concerns over how much power the states have and how the states use their power. The easiest thing to do would be to collect taxes as a percentage of the means of payments used in all kinds of transactions, both in the financial economy and the real economy, and to abolish all other types of taxes and levies. Then it will be up to the governments to decide if they want to exchange what they collect into other types of money.

Those who argue that such a reform will raise practical problems too large to consider, in my view ignore the fact that there are many things that have been difficult to accomplish. For instance, we managed to send people to the moon, although it was extremely difficult, and at the time it was not clear what good it would do for humankind. If the Netherlands could reinstall monetary freedom in the 16th century, the advances in technology and innovations that we have had since then indicate that it should be a lot easier for us to carry out such reforms today. The fact that it will require resources and take time are not strong enough arguments against reestablishing monetary freedom.

Expectedly, politicians will argue that reforming the monetary system requires international cooperation. One thing is certain: this will come at the cost of delays and global electioneering. Experience demonstrates that monetary freedom is even more valuable for a country if all the other countries have unsound money, because the flow of money and capital to the country with monetary freedom becomes even greater. There are enormous advantages for those who make the first move. At the same time – for each new nation that introduces sound money, the risk of hyperinflation will increase for all the other nations, and especially for the US.

Whether the new monetary system is a centralized or a decentralized system, there is reason to believe that it will be based upon gold. We have seen the BRICS countries discussing the possibility of using "a basket of commodities and national currencies" as backing for a common currency, an idea that I believe to be deeply flawed. It sounds like someone is trying to design a system that can be manipulated in the same way as it was with the quasi gold standards of the 20th century.

**Transition phase, planning and action**
Both citizens and governments will have to make plans for a transition process to the new monetary system.

Politicians need to define the *end goal* and how long a *time* the transition phase should be and ensure that the transition happens *gradually* to allow people and businesses to adapt. New Zealand did not abolish fiat money but made sweeping reforms in several economic sectors in the 1980s. The fact that successive governments, both conservative and liberal, have maintained a strong commitment to these reforms, is a testament to the success of it as a policy. It is likely that much can be learned from New Zealand, also in terms of identifying what that could be executed even better.

The way I see it, the only alternative to preparing for a transition to a new monetary system would be to wait for the current system to end in hyperinflation and political turmoil, and hope that something good would appear in its stead.

**What you can do yourself**
Learning more and sharing the knowledge is the most important thing. The website *mises.org* is dedicated to providing information about the Austrian school of economics and is a good place to start. In my experience, you can also learn more about economics and economic policy from selected podcasts than from the mass media.

Those who join a political party are given the opportunity to influence monetary policy directly. In Norway, for example, only 3% of the population are members of a political party, and of these, only a small proportion are politically active. This means that the odds of achieving a real change in monetary policy are quite high if you legitimately get involved. You don't have to become a politician yourself. But from the inside, you can influence what the party policies should be, who should be nominated and position yourself to talk directly to the political leaders.

Brexit and the elections in 2022 in Sweden and Italy, won by nationalist conservative parties Sverigedemokratene and Fratelli d'Italia, and the growing support for right-wing conservative Marine Le Pen's Rassemblement National in France, signals that the electorate want significant changes. In Sweden the support for Sverigedemokratene almost doubled among voters aged between 18 and 21 who were voting for the very first time, as it increased from 12 to 22%, according to Swedish Television's exit poll. In Italy 23% of this age group supported Fratelli d'Italia. The political establishment has in general been strong supporters of globalism, aggressive climate change policies as well as harsh measures during the COVID-19 pandemic. The youngest voters were the demographic hardest hit by the lockdown. It is my interpretation that the political elite increasingly has lost the people's trust and that the youth wants change. I believe that we just have seen the beginning of this development, and that the inflation policy and the economic crisis will function as a powerful catalyst.

We may also learn something from the following three observations which refer to some of the developments that we have looked at previously in this book:

(1) Foreign coins with high silver content, disappeared to other countries after Harald Hardråde started his inflation scheme in the 11th century. The reason was most likely that some other countries still had monetary freedom, and that these countries became the recipients of "the good money". Today we have fiat money regimes all over the world, which means that silver and gold coins probably will not obey Greshams law, at least not to the same extent. We should also remember that it is not a criminal act to use something else than the state's currency in voluntary transactions.

(2) Following the revolution in the Netherlands in the 16$^{th}$ century, people appreciated their monetary freedom, understood its true value and therefore were able to enjoy a long period of economic growth. Although modern day society is plagued with fiat money, we have the opportunity to use silver, gold, and cryptocurrency as mediums of exchange. But we must understand the true value of monetary freedom to be able to make the transition from idea to action.

(3) It is not only technical innovation that defines the Bitcoin success. The success is primarily that the Bitcoin movement has become an unstoppable vehicle for the growth and distribution of the following idea: That we cannot have individual freedom if we use a monetary system that is controlled by the government. I believe that an increasingly large group of Bitcoiners have now come to realize what the Trønders probably understood sometime after Harald Hardråde set up his mint in Trondheim in 1050. I see the Bitcoin movement as a movement that rediscovers a lost freedom.

These three observations teach us that we have everything to gain from being open minded when someone offers to pay with something other than fiat money. They also teach us that we should start to inform others that we are *monetary agnostics* ourselves. The value of making a habit of saying "I would be glad to take payment in silver, gold or Bitcoin, if that is more convenient to you", and to use other types of money than the nation's currency when giving away presents cannot be overestimated. One can easily find the price of, for instance gold and Bitcoin, on the Internet, something which facilitates using other means of payment than fiat money.

In a modern economy that functions adequately and appropriately, this cannot *replace* fiat money, but getting used to spending and having alternative means of payment will make both businesses and citizens less vulnerable. Sneer if you will. However, when the Norwegian government explains that they are now urging people to keep some cash, and that they require the business community to accept cash, by saying that we must be prepared if the electronic payment systems break down, it is reasonable to heed the warning. If something this catastrophic happens, cash fiat money will quickly fall in value, and then it is important to have alternative means of payment at hand.

By far the most important thing, however, is to teach young people about the dangers of inflation before society begins to indoctrinate them with the belief that it is both necessary and good for them to incur debt.

**Central banks' and politicians' handling of high price inflation**

European central banks caused enormous damage to the real economy with their parity policies in the 1920s and the substantial interest rate increases after the crash in 1987. There were too many who had borrowed too much, and they could not handle the combination of interest rate increases and having to repay with money that was significantly more valuable than the money they had borrowed.

Today, the economy is based on debt to a much greater extent. If governments do not take substantial action at the same time as central banks curb growth in the money supply, the damage to the real economy is likely to be *considerably greater* in 2022 than it was in the 1920s and after 1987. Substantial tax cuts appear to be the only option when interest rates continue to rise. *This means that the public sector must be scaled down significantly*. There are two problems with this. Firstly, it is difficult to get politicians to reduce taxes. Secondly, there is a widespread misconception among economists that tax cuts create what they call *inflationary pressure*. This is because they do not understand that it is an increase in the money supply that is the driver. Additionally, governments have a nasty little habit of spending money on rate comparable to its citizens.

It is therefore more likely than not that central banks and governments will choose the most harmful solution, i.e., a period of high interest rates, high taxes, and high prices – with a real economy that is completely unbidden and on its knees. It doesn't have to be this way, but if the advisers tell politicians that taxes must not be touched, then this eventuality is almost guaranteed.

# Saving and investing

**Introduction**

We will now look at saving and investing in an economy characterized by inflation. But firstly, lets address some definitions. In economics, a distinction is made between consumption, savings and investments.

*Consumption* is the same as using up wealth, in whole or in part. *Saving* is the same as not consuming wealth. You set it aside so that you can use it or invest it later. *Investing* is the same as placing economic resources in a way that allows you to make a profit, for example in the form of interest on a bank deposit, rental income from an apartment, dividends from a company or a surplus as result of a difference between the price you pay when you buy something and what your return is when you sell it. To make a profit, one must in principle take a chance, thusly there is a risk that one can also lose that investment. The greater the risk of loss, the greater the potential profit must be.

**Traditional savings**

Most people are aware that it is currently not possible to use fiat money for saving. Price inflation eats up the value, even if you put it in an interest-bearing account at the bank. Among other things, this has led people to take up huge loans to become homeowners and buying holiday houses. Many economists call this "savings" and there is significant political stimulation of home ownership in many countries, especially in Norway and the US. To call ordinary citizens buying frenzy in the inflation-driven property market "saving" is problematic in many ways. There is no other expression that is more adequate for this than the time-honored statement: "you cannot have your cake and eat it". Buying your own home and holiday home is primarily consumption. It has also been some sort of investment, but in recent years this has turned into outright speculation.

Secondly, the real estate crashes in 1987 and in connection with the financial crisis in 2008 show that house prices take a significant hit after the credit bubbles have burst. In these instances, the price decline in Norway averaged 8-9% per year. With this tempo house prices lose almost half the value in six years and with the debt-to-income ratio that people have today, it blows away all the equity for many of those who believe that they have saved in housing. This shows that to the extent that debt-financed home purchases are something else in addition to consumption – it is investment with a not-so-insignificant element of risk, and certainly not a form of saving.

If we now experience a sharp decline in house prices, this will be the third time in Norway in the last 35 years. Considering that people depend on having a place to live, and that they have borrowed up to the hilt to become owners, there is every reason to conclude that many have taken much too great a risk.

**Saving in gold and silver**

Today, gold and silver appear to be the only real alternatives for saving. Gold has had the most stable purchasing power, but silver has also been used since the early upright bi-peds postulated transactions, both as a means of payment and for saving. The advantage of silver is that silver coins cost less and can be used for smaller transactions, even for change, compared with gold coins. The disadvantage of silver is that the rate of extraction is higher, i.e., that the amount of silver increases more and that purchasing power decreases faster compared with gold.

Allocating some of one's savings in physical gold and silver is also an insurance policy against inflation and will be particularly valuable if the monetary system implodes.

In the introduction, we looked at the development of the purchasing power of the krone and the dollar in relation to the official statistics on the cost of living, which showed that the value of the krone was 65 times higher in 1913, the year before the lifting of the gold standard in Norway, compared with 2022, while the value of the dollar at that time was 30 times higher. If we look at the redemption values at that time, which were 100 NOK for 40 grams of gold, and 20.67 USD for 1 ounce (30.13 grams) of gold and compare it with gold prices in the spot market at the time of writing, the krone was 220 times more valuable in 1913 than it is today, while the dollar was 82 times more valuable. This is yet another example of gold retaining its purchasing power over time to a much greater extent than fiat money.

Small transaction costs are incurred when trading coins with professional gold and silver dealers. As more people become coin owners and a larger private market becomes a reality, transaction costs might fall. If many start using silver or gold coins, they may even trade at a premium compared to fiat money. As with everything else, owning gold isn't 100% risk-free. The risk of theft entails costs for safe storage. History also shows that governments have confiscated gold. France and the United States confiscated their own citizens' gold in 1720 and 1933, respectively. Lenin did the same in the Soviet Union and Mussolini in Italy. Germany confiscated gold wholesale, nationwide during World War II, as would all invasion forces do given half the chance. This is not something that is easy to hedge against, but on the other hand, it is something that happens infrequently.

If governments revert to some sort of gold standard in combination with well-functioning electronic money, leaving the money in the account may once more become the traditional way to save money again. Meanwhile, perhaps companies such as *Goldmoney* and *Gold Switzerland* offer a solution. According to their websites they sell gold that they store for their customers in the customers' name, with insurance, audit, and the possibility to transfer ownership between its customers.

There are large fluctuations in the prices of cryptocurrencies, which denotes a higher risk. Therefore, buying cryptocurrency is not by definition saving, as it must be considered as an *investment*.

Anyone who wants to combine saving and protesting against the current fiat money system should, in my opinion, buy silver or gold instead of putting money into cryptocurrency.

**Investing**

Since saving in fiat money is not possible, people are instead driven towards taking risks. It means that they feel compelled to invest to keep the purchasing power of their money. It works like this:

Price inflation of 2% turns savings into a loss in accounts with a deposit interest rate of 1%. So, you may place the money in fixed income funds with the expectation of four percent instead, even if you then also run a certain risk that you may lose money. If price inflation then reaches, for example, 5%, this also means that you lose money. Therefore, you jump into the stock market, where the risk is higher, so you need a return of at least 8-9% for it to be justifiable. If inflation reaches 8-9%, as it is now in the EU and the US, one must either concede defeat and accept negative returns or take the plunge into speculation with even higher risk, for example in the market for unlisted stocks. The more people trapped in this vicious circle, and the higher the inflation is, fewer become real winners, something ably proven with the German hyperinflation experience.

The securities market is not for amateurs. This is even more true when the bubbles have begun to burst, and markets fluctuate widely. Many have large mortgages while they at the same time invest in equities in the hope that the market fluctuations are already over. It may be a good reminder that both Keynes and Fisher lost their wealth on the stock exchange in 1929, even though they were in a significantly better position to influence market developments and know what was going on than the majority of us.

The cryptocurrency market has all the characteristics that a speculation market caused by inflation tends to have, not least that it has weak or no connection to the real economy. I am not equipped enough to comment on whether it might make sense to invest in cryptocurrency or whether, for example, Bitcoin is good and other cryptocurrencies are bad. However, parts of the cryptocurrency market, such as speculation in tokens that can be used for speculation in a virtual world, make investing in tulip bulb future contracts and shares in a French-owned trading company run by a convicted murderer and professional gambler seem a safe bet.

Gold retains stability in its value over time but does not generate a return. Gold is therefore not something that one normally invests in. In a crisis, however, one would expect gold to rise more in value than most other financial resources. If governments reintroduce the gold standard or let the people decide freely what they want to spend as money, it will also mean that the demand for gold increases. Normally, increased demand would also mean that gold increases in value compared to all other things. Buying gold can therefore be regarded as both a saving and a speculative investment in relation to the possibility of a major economic crisis or a new monetary system linked to gold.

There are several investors who believe that the fiat system is already on borrowed time. Jim Rogers and Peter Schiff are two of the best known in this category, and they have long argued that it is the commodity market that may be the most profitable market to invest in. Since the inflation economy favors both securities, real estate, and entities that sell consumer goods more than commodities, an end to fiat money as a policy may cause commodities to rise in value compared to much everything else. From this perspective, investing in farmland also appears interesting. In Norway, however, the planned agricultural policy makes investment in the agricultural sector appear to be a high-risk endeavor. Being a farmer today is something reserved for the purists and idealists, those who are fully aware that what they are doing is tantamount to financial insanity, top to bottom.

# How to cope with the inflation economy

Now that we have gone through what inflation is and how it affects society and people, we can look at how individuals and families can cope with the inflation economy. We will distinguish between the centralized and the decentralized model.

In the centralized model, you stay as close to the fiat money source as possible. Then you move to the big city and get a job in the financial industry. You take out as much loan as possible within the risk you can live with, without assuming personal responsibility for the debt. The money must be invested continuously. To succeed, you must conduct your business through a company with limited liability. The centralized model focuses on maximizing economic wealth by taking the least possible personal risk, through utilizing credit, and increasing your paper values.

In the decentralized model, you remove yourself as far away from the source of new money as possible. Typically, you move to the countryside and do as much as you can on your own, both when it comes to getting a roof over your head and food on the table. You do not take out loans, you barter, and you trade in the private secondary market as much as possible. It is important to demonstrate to the other actors in the marketplace that you are willing to accept other mediums of exchange, for instance Bitcoin, silver and gold, and not only the nation's currency.

The decentralized model is all about living a good life with less consumption, while renouncing many of the goods and services that most people in modern society chase after. You save in silver and gold, which can be bought at an artificially low price in an inflation-based economy. When you have set aside sufficient savings, you can invest some of the surplus in bitcoin or capital that gives a real economic return without building up large and complex production structures.

The decentralized model can be economically beneficial. In a country that is based on fiat money, there are many real economic resources that it is impossible for fiat money to suck away from the countryside. Plots of land and old houses can be bought for a pittance and nothing. The inflation economy causes means of production to become obsolete long before they are worn out. They can be obtained for free or cheaply and often have a lot of remaining life that can be used for small-scale production. Wood can be cut for free in return for clearing the edges of farmland for the farmers. You can grow much of what you need on your own property in large parts of Norway, alternatively you can rent plots of land which the farmers leave fallow almost free of charge. Hunting and fishing are almost free in many places in Norway, and gathering mushrooms, berries, herbs, and much more is absolutely free for everyone. Solar cell technology is becoming affordable and can supply all the electricity you need for lighting and charging various equipment. Internet connection costs little, and home offices have become common, so that you can have a well-paid job without living in the city. This is the case in many other places in the world too, not just in Norway. With a little knowledge and patience, you can become financially independent without going into debt.

You do not have to choose either the centralized or the decentralized model. For example, someone who feels trapped in the inflation economy can start by reducing consumption and moving some of the unspent fiat money into silver and gold coins as well as Bitcoin. Just knowing that you own something that has a lasting and stable value gives you the feeling that you are creating a new platform and removing yourself a bit from the inflation economy. Anyone who owns a cottage by the sea can sell it and instead buy a small farm in the countryside. There are many ways to bring about a gradual transition to a new and more free existence where inflation affects daily life to a lesser extent.

# Conclusion

In the almost 1,000 years that have passed since Harald Hardråde introduced the death penalty to coerce people into using his coins, we have learned that monetary inflation is all about state power, fraud, war, centralization, and most importantly: an enormous redistribution of wealth.

We have also learned that economists, politicians and citizens are misled, as they focus mainly on the *consequences* of the inflation policy – price increases – and that they lose sight of the fact that it is the expansion of the money supply that is the underlying cause. These are the reasons why the "government may secretly and unobserved, confiscate the wealth of the people, and not one man in a million will detect the theft", as Keynes stated.

Instead of solving the underlying problem, politicians and economists try to combat the price increases with price caps, rationing, export prohibitions and other measures that gets more and more extreme and that only exacerbates the problems. In the worst case, these policies end in hyperinflation and political upheaval.

A fundamental prerequisite for society to accelerate rapidly in the direction of a global inflation policy was that economics was radically transformed. Keynes, Fisher, and Frisch created a quasi-scientific basis for money printing.

The very negative economic and social development that we have had after the states moved away from the gold standard shows that the argument that inflation is positive for economic development is obviously invalid, and that it is without a doubt a dangerous theory.

The question is whether the claim that inflation is good for *politics* can be correct. This really says it all:

- Global debt increased by 70% in 2020 to 2021
- We have a global food and power crisis at the same time as the digital economy grows two and a half times as fast as the rest of the economy
- The wealthiest get a lot wealthier, and the government grows a lot bigger at the expense of the rest of society

The inflation policy is primarily the result of deliberate actions of many people over a long period of time. However, the actions had consequences that mainly the economists from the Austrian school were able to foresee. Helped by the financial elite and economists who wanted to be social engineers, the politicians chose to close their ears to the warnings they received.

Nobody should be surprised that this is the way it goes when someone decides that it is good for all of us if we create new money out of nothing. Looking back, we can only wonder how we failed to understand that it was a total sham, a kind of alchemy in disguise. When the politicians, financial elite, and academics with the most influence in their lack of knowledge and wisdom chose inflation as a policy, it was as if they unleashed a virus. What is most dangerous now are two things: Almost none of the politicians understand what has happened and absolutely no one wants to take the responsibility of getting the world out of the problem.

As we have seen, anyone who understands what inflation is about will have great advantages, even if you just want to avoid the disadvantages of the inflation economy.

I choose to believe that one day we will get to decide for ourselves which money we want to use. It's not going to happen automatically. It will require rational thinking, commitment, courage, prudence, and a will for peaceful debate if we are to make this becoming a reality.

If we are to succeed, we absolutely have to focus on **the big picture** and empower our youth to learn about the history of inflation policy.

# Afterword

I hope that you have benefited from reading the book. If you have concluded that:

- unlike other economic resources, the total amount of fiat money does not become more valuable as the amount of money increases
- the longer time passes while the supply of fiat money increases, and the faster it grows, the less freedom we are left with, and the greater the redistribution of wealth becomes
- it is possible for both citizens and states to opt out of the inflation economy, in whole or in part
- there will be great advantages to abolishing states' monopolies on money and re-establishing monetary freedom.

then you have understood the most important aspects of this subject.

If you have also understood why Harald Hardråde saw it necessary to kill the Trønder Earl Einar Tambarskjelve and his son Eindride to succeed with his inflation scheme in Norway, and that all of us would need to forget this lesson in order for a group of progressive academics to be able to convince everyone that it was a scientific fact that inflation creates wealth, you have come a long way.

I believe that my ancestors quickly felt the harsh consequences of the inflation policy, and that they understood the direction in which it was going. Hopefully the book can inspire some readers to find out when and why monetary freedom was abolished where they live.

Last, but not least, we must realize that monetary freedom is an important part of our heritage. It should remind us that the goal should be to abolish inflation policy, not to design a new monetary system.

If you have any comments or questions, please feel free to contact me. You can find out how at www.libertus.no.

Seek the truth.

R.Ø.

# Bibliography

Amadeo, K. (2022), *Who Owns the U.S. National Debt?* TheBalance.com

Applebaum, B. (2019), *America's Most Profitable Export: Money,* NYTimes.com

Atkeson, A. et al (2004), *Deflation and Depression: Is There an Empirical Link? Economists*, Federal Reserve Bank of Minneapolis

Bandlien B., et al (2022), *The Battle of Stiklestad*, SNL.no

Bank of England (2020), *Why does money depend on trust?* Bankofengland.co.uk

Bankenes sikringsfond, *Årsrapport 2021*, Bankenessikringsfond.no

Bjerkholt O. (2018), *Memorandum: Ragnar Frisch (1895-1973)*, University of Oslo

Bjørke, C. N., et al (2018), *A Norwegian village knows who killed Karl XII*, Nrk.no

Board of Governors of The Federal Reserve System (2020), *Reserve requirements*, Federalreserve.gov

Boston Consulting Group (2022), *Global Wealth Grew by Double Digits to $530 Trillion in 2021, Despite Continued Crises*, Bcg.com

Boyle, P. (2021), *John Law – The First Financial Engineer – A History of Paper Money and the Mississippi Bubble*, Spotify

Breuninger, K. (2019), *Trump rails against Powell a day after the Fed cuts rates for a third time this year*, CNBC.com

Burnham, T. (2014) *Is your money safe at the bank?* Pbs.org

Cantillon, R. (1755), *An Essay on Economic Theory,* Mises.org

Chestney, N (2022), Global carbon markets value surged to record $851 billion last year, Reuters.com

de Soto, H. (2003), *The Mystery of Capital*, Basic Books

DiLella, C. et al (2022), *Investors are paying millions for virtual land in the metaverse*, CNBC.com

Eagle, J (2021), *Here's How Reserve Currencies Have Evolved Over 120 Years*, Visualcapitalist.com

Federal Deposit Insurance Corporation (2014), *Deposit insurance at a glance*, Fdic.gov

Federal Reserve Bank of New York, *Maiden Lane Transactions*, Newyorkfed.org

Federal Reserve Bank of St. Louis (2022), *Value Added by Industry*, fred.stlouisfed.org

Federal Reserve Bank of St. Louis, *Median Sales Price of Houses Sold for the United States*

Ferguson A. (1975), *When Money Dies: The Nightmare of the Weimar Collapse*, William Kimber

Filatochev I. et al (1992), *The Soviet Hyperinflation: Its Origins and Impact throughout the Former Republics*, Taylor & Francis, Ltd.

Fisher, I. N. (1956), *My father, Irving Fisher (A Reflection book)*, Comet

Frank, R. (2022), *Soaring markets helped the richest 1% gain $6.5 trillion in wealth last year, according to the Fed*, CNBC.com

French, D. E. (1992), *Early Speculative Bubbles and Increases in the Supply of Money,* Mises Institute
French, D. E. (1992), *Early Speculative Bubbles and Increases in the Supply of Money,* Mises Institute
French, D. E. (2014), *The Dutch Monetary Environment During Tulipmania, Mises.org*

Friedman, M. et al (1963), A Monetary History of the United States, 1867-1960, Princeton University Press

Frisby, D. (2022), China almost certainly owns more gold than the US – here's why that matters, moneyweek.com

Geber, M. (2019), *The Art of Creating Money in the Modern Economy*, NHH Brage

Gerdrup, K. R., *The Norwegian Banking crises ch. 5, Three booms and busts involving banking crises in Norway since the 1890s*, Norges Bank's Occasional Papers

Gibbon, E. (1776), *Decline and Fall of the Roman Empire, W. Strahan and T. Cadell*
Gibbon, E. (1776), *Decline and Fall of the Roman Empire, W. Strahan and T. Cadell*
Gjedrem, S. (2004), *Monetary Policy and the Economic Development*, Norges-bank.no

Goldgar, A (2008), *Tulipmania: Money, Honor and Knowledge in the Dutch Golden Age,* University of

Granath, A. (2022), *Central Banks Claim to Preserve the Value of Money through Inflation.* Mises.org

Gullbekk (2009), S. H., *Coinage as Source of Income in the Middle Age, Academia.edu*

Gullbekk, S. H. (1994), *Norwegian Coinage in the Early Middle Ages: Organisering av Myntvesenet og Myntenes funksjon ca 1050-1100,* Duo.uio.no

Gundersen, G. I. et al (2021), *The Number of Business Entities in Agriculture fell by 17 percent the past ten Years*, SSB.no

Hanisch, T. J. et al (2005), *The Forgotten Dissertation: Trygve J.B. Hoff, "Economic Calculation in the Socialist Society"*, Fabrizio Serra Editore, Pisa – Roma

Hayek. F. A. (1974), *The Pretence of Knowledge*, Nobeliprize.org

Hazlitt, H. (1964) *What You should know about Inflation*, D. van Nostrand Company, Inc.

Hewitt, Mike (2008), *Hyperinflation in China*, Dollardaze.org

Hoff, T. J. B (1938), *Economic Calculation in Socialist Societies*, Aschehoug

Hoover, H. (1952), *The Memoirs of Herbert Hoover*, Macmillan

Hülsmann, Jörg Guido Mises (2007), *The Last Knight of Liberalism*, Mises Institute

Høgseth, Martin Hagh (2022), *The ECB surprises with med double interest rate hike*, e24.no

Keynes, J. M. (1919), *The Economic Consequences of the Peace*

Keynes, J. M. (1933), From Keynes to Roosevelt: Our Recovery Plan assayed, New York Times

Keynes, J. M. (1936), *The General Theory on Money, Interest and Employment*, MacMillan
Kharpal, A. (2022), *Crypto firms say thousands of digital currencies will collapse, compare market to early dotcom days*, CNBC.com
Kloster, A. (2019), *How is Money made?* Norges-bank.no
Kloster, A. (2020), *QE og Helicopter Money – what is the Difference?* Norges-bank.no
Ladstein, et al (2005), *The development of the Agriculture Sector in Norway 950-2005*, SSB.no
Lobo, D. (2015), *Albert Edwards: Yellen - the new 'economic war criminal*, Citywire.com
Mellemstrand, C. (2022), *Has so much debt that I feel hands and feet tied*, Nationen.no
Mikkelborg, G. (2022), *Oil price 1946 – 2021 in NOK and grams of gold per barrel*, Gullerpenger.no
Mullis, M. E. (2021), *Staten eser ut: Norge topper internasjonal kåring*, Nettavisen.no
Morkinskinna, (1220), tales of the Norwegian Kings 1035 – 1157
Murphy, R. *(2021), The Bob Murphy Show ep. January 17th, 2021,* Spotify
Nakamoto, S. (2008), *Bitcoin: A Peer-to-Peer Electronic Cash System*, Bitcoin.org
Nicolaisen, J. (2017), *Hva skal våre penger være?* Norges-bank.no
Nordbakken, L. P. (2019), *Trygve J. B. Hoff: the authorship*, Civita
Nordbø, E. (2014), *Fra gull til KPI. Pengepolitikken og prisutviklingen gjennom 100 år*, Statistics Norway
Norges Bank (2004), *Norges Bank has sold parts of its gold reserves*, Norges-bank.no
Norges Lover (2015), *Finansforetaksloven* Lovdata.no
O'Neill, A. (2021), *Ratio of government expenditure to gross domestic product (GDP) in the United States from 2017 to 2027*, Statista.com
OECD (2019), *Health and social care workforce*, Oecd-ilibrary.org
Olsen, Ø. (2017), *The Monetary Policy's objective and scope,* Norges-bank.no
Opstad L. (2020), *Introduction to Macroeconomics*, Cappelen Damm
Pistilli, M. (2022), *Top 10 Central Bank Gold Holdings (Updated 2022)*, Investingnews.com
Putin, V. (2022), *Speech at the St. Petersburg's International Economic Forum,* Kremlin.ru
Reinert E. (2008), *How Rich Countries Got Rich*, Constable and Robinson
Riedel, B (2020), *75 years after a historic meeting on the USS Quincy, US-Saudi relations are in need of a true re-think*, Brookings Institute
Rothbard, M. (1963), *America's Great Depression*, Mises Institute
Rothbard, M. (1963), *What has government done to our money?* Mises Institute
Rothbard, M. (1988), *Nine myths about the crash*, Mises.org

Rothbard, M. (2002) *The History of Money and Banking in the United States*, Mises Institute

Rygg, N (1918) *Norges Bank's History, part 1*, Riksarkivet

Salerno, J. (2000), *Biography of Carl Menger: The Founder of the Austrian School (1840-1921)*, Mises Institute

Seim, D. L. (2007), *Perhaps we can hit upon some medium of course: Rockefeller philanthropy, economic research, and the structure of social science – 1911-1946*, Iowa State University

Slotten, A. (2021), *Did you think that the wealth gap was small in Norway?* NRK.no

Smialek, J (2020), *Trump Says He Could Demote Fed Chair Powell, Risking More Market Turmoil*, NYTimes.com

Smith, A. (1776), *Wealth of Nations*

Smith, E. et al (1998), *Report from the Commission of Inquiry to Stortinget*

St. Lous Fed (2022), *M2 (M2SL)*, Fred.stlouisfed.org

Statistics Norway (1965), *The Norwegian economy after the war from 1965*, SSB.no

Statistics Norway (2022), *Konsumprisindeksen*, SSB.no

Sturlasson, S. (13th century), *The Sagas of the Viking Kings of Norway – Heimskringla*

Størkson, O. E. et al (2019), *The Rescue of the Norwegian Gold*, NRK.no

*Sæther A.*, et al. (2014), *Ragnar Frisch and the Postwar Norwegian Economy by*, Econ Journal Watch

Sættem, J. B. et al (2012), *This is how Housing Prices have developed the last 200 Years*, NRK.no

Teigen, C. (2015), *Did you know that the Money you borrow didn't exist previously?* Finansavisen.no

The International Monetary Fund (2021), *Global Debt Reaches a Record $226 Trillion*, IMF.org

The International Monetary Fund (2022), *World Economic Outlook Update July 2022*, IMF.org

The World Bank (2022), *Digital Development*, Worldbank.org

Thomassen, E. (2014), *Financial power – people power, the Labor Party and the demand for democratization of Norges Bank approx. 1920–49*

Titlestad, T (2016), *Viking Age, Resistance Law and Democracy,* Saga Bok

Toje, A. (2022), *Europe's slips unnoticeably into Decay*, AsleToje.no

Tradingeconomics.com (2022), *various commodity prices*

Trondsen, F. (2008), *Now the scientists know who killed Karl XII*, Aftenposten.no

Turk J. (2021), *Money and Liberty,* Wood Lane Books

U.S. Bureau of Labor Statistics, *CPI Inflation Calculator,* Data.bls.gov

US Government Spending (2021), *US Government Spending History from 1900*, Usgovernmentspending.com

US.Debt.Clock.org

Von Mises, L. (1912), *The Theory of Money and Credit*, Mises Institute

Von Mises, L. (1944), *Omnipotent Government: The Rise of the Total State and Total War*, Yale University

Von Mises, L. (1949), *Human Action: A Treatise on Economics*, Mises Institute

Wasik, J. F. (2013), *John Maynard Keynes's Way to Wealth*, McGraw-Hill Education

Wetterberg, G, (2018), *Money and Power, the Book about the History of Riksbanken*, Sveriges Riksbank

Wilkes, T. (2022), *Emerging markets drive global debt to record $303 trillion* – IIF, Reuters.com

Wong, A. (2016), *The Untold Story Behind Saudi Arabia's 41-Year U.S. Debt Secret*, Bloomberg.com

World Gold Council (2021), *Above-ground Stocks,* Gold.org

I would like to give special thanks to the Mises Institute for working tirelessly to educate the world on everything related to economics, to Gregard Mikkelborg for all the discussions we have had on everything about inflation, to Lars M. Haugen, for providing me with valuable input after he read a draft of the manuscript, and my sister Ingrid Elise Østgård and her partner Scott Baker-Marflitt for all the help they have given me with the translation of the book into English. If there are any errors in the book, it is solely my responsibility.

R.Ø.

# Inflation policy timeline

# (The author's perspective)

**431 BCE:** Athens finances the Peloponnesian War with inflation by reducing the amount of gold and silver in their coins so they can produce more coins.

**414 BCE:** Athens loses the Peloponnesian War.

**404 BCE:** Athens surrenders after being besieged by Spartan military forces.

**Around years 100-476 AD:** The emperors of the Roman Empire gradually reduce the silver content of their coins from 95% at the transition from the first to the second century to 0.5% in year 268. The Roman Empire is at its greatest under the emperor Trajan in year 117, but begins to disintegrate in the third century, before splitting in two in 386. The Western Roman Empire falls in 476.

**950-960:** Håkon the Good of Norway ensures that the Frostating Law, which has been handed down orally through generations, is written down. The law applies in Trøndelag in central Norway and has the following warning: "With law the country will be built, and with unlaw it will be destroyed." Unlike all the other Nordic laws, it also has a rule that everyone has the right and duty to pursue and, if possible, kill the king, if he extorts property without the Frostating's approval.

**1020:** Widespread monetary inflation due to banknote production during the S'ung Dynasty in China.

**1028:** The Trønders have grown tired of Olav Haraldsson, later to become St. Olav, and his abuse of power. King Knut of Denmark helps them chase him and his men out of the country.

**1030:** Olav Haraldsson and his half-brother Harald Sigurdsson arrives with an army to try and take back Norway. The Trønder peasant army wins. Torstein Knarresmed, Tore Hund and Kalv Arnesson kill Olav, while Harald is injured and flee.

**Around 1035:** Harald Sigurdsson, later nicknamed Hardråde, arrives in Constantinople, the capital of the Eastern Roman Empire, where he and his men join the emperor's personal guard. He learns how the emperor uses inflation to build up power.

**1046:** Harald Hardråde returns and becomes the new King of Norway.

**1050:** Harald Hardråde kills the Trønder chief Einar Tambarskjelve and his son Eindride in a cowardly plot. In the same year, Harald sets up mints in Nidaros and Hamar and decides that those who do not accept his coins can be punished with death.

**1066:** The silver content in Harald's coins has been reduced from around 90% to 33%. He sets out from Norway with more than 200 ships and somewhere between 7 and 9,000 men to conquer England. King Harold Godwinson and his army surprise Harald and the soldiers encamped at Stamford Bridge. Harald's army is slaughtered, and he himself dies from an arrow that hits him in the throat. The Viking era is now over.

**1166:** Hyperinflation due to widespread banknote issuance during the Chin Dynasty of China.

**1296:** Marco Polo returns to Europe and tells the Europeans about the monetary policy he has seen in China. People are at pains to believe he was telling the truth.

**1555:** Revolution in the Netherlands. The state reforms the monetary system, and silver and gold flood in from countries that practice inflation policy, and the Netherlands eventually ends up becoming Europe's leading trading country.

**1657:** Johan Palmstruch earns the right to set up Stockholm Banco, in exchange for King Charles X of Sweden receiving a share of the profits.

**1663:** People rush to Stockholm Banco to get their money, after Palmstruch has created chaos with banknote printing and large loans, including to the Swedish King.

**1668:** Riksens Ständers Bank, the world's first central bank, is set up in Stockholm, Sweden. The bank eventually creates money out of nothing and becomes the King's personal wallet.

**1709:** The Swedish warrior King Charles XII, who had previously defeated Russia and Poland and won the Great Nordic War, is decisively defeated by the Russian army at the Battle of Poltava in Ukraine.

**1709:** People rush to Riksens Ständers Bank to get their money, after the bank has created chaos with banknote printing and large loans, especially to Charles XII.

**1715:** Sweden is on the brink of bankruptcy, and Charles XII orders the production of "emergency coins" to finance the state's expenses.

**1718:** Charles XII has brought 40,000 men from Sweden with him to subjugate Norway. In Halden, he dies from a head shot. The Swedes give up.

**1719-1720:** John Law succeeds in getting the French government to ban all money other than banknotes and to confiscate all the gold in France.

**1720:** John Law's paper money experiment in France ends abruptly, in what is called history's first financial bubble.

**1787:** The delegates who draft the US Constitution meet. Several argue that inflation is a crime against humanity.

**1792:** The US Congress passes the Coinage Act. It stipulates that an employee or official at the mint who fraudulently creates coins with a lower weight or with less silver or gold than what the law prescribes shall be punished with death.

**1816:** The Norwegian Storting decides to establish Norges Bank.

**1913:** A group of financiers, bureaucrats, politicians, and academics succeed in convincing Congress to set up a central banking system in the US.

**1914:** There is war in Europe and one country after another breaks its promise to let its citizens redeem notes for gold.

**1917:** Lenin uses hyperinflation as a weapon to destroy the capitalists and make it easier for the communists to gain control of the means of production. Famine breaks out, millions of people die.

**1919-28:** Norges Bank shrinks the money supply in what is called *parity policy*, causing an enormous economic downturn with bankruptcies and persistently high unemployment.

**1921-23:** Hyperinflation in Germany.

**1925-28:** The Bank of England and The Federal Reserve conspire to persuade other countries to join a gold exchange standard, which will allow the British and Americans to expand their currencies.

**1927-1928:** Ragnar Frisch, who has obtained his doctorate in statistics at the University of Oslo, is on a research stay in the USA, funded by a scholarship from the Rockefeller Foundation.

**1928:** Norway and several other countries enter a gold exchange standard with the Bank of England in the driver's seat.

**1929:** Stock market crash, including in London and New York.

**1930-31:** Frisch is on another stay in the USA. He gets to know Professor Irving Fisher and is offered a professorship at Yale University.

**1931:** Gold exchange standard No. 1 collapses as the British stop the redemption of pounds for gold. The UK is technically bankrupt and in breach of international obligations.

**1932:** Frisch has declined the offer from Yale. With support from the Rockefeller Foundation, Frisch sets up the first economic institute in Norway and is appointed professor by the Storting. The foundation finances several dozen employees who form the basis for Frisch's work. Frisch begins the work of convincing the politicians of the superiority of the planned economy and requests that the state introduce a more expansive monetary policy.

**1933:** Professor Fisher is relieved. In a letter to his wife, he writes that he has saved the family from ruin by convincing President Roosevelt to go off the gold standard and to expand the money supply.

**1936:** The book *The General Theory of Employment, Interest and Money* by British economist John Maynard Keynes is published. Keynes argues that inflation has a positive effect on the economy.

**1944:** Bretton Woods, New Hampshire, USA: 44 countries, including the US, Canada, the Soviet Union and China agree on a second gold exchange standard, with a common exchange rate, and the right for all other central banks to demand that the US central bank redeem 35 USD for an ounce of gold.

**1945:** Roosevelt meets Saudi Arabian head of state King Abdul Aziz Ibn Saud to discuss strategic cooperation for the post-war era.

**1946:** The Soviet Union will not ratify the Bretton Woods Agreement, which they believe is directed by the financial elite of Wall Street, New York.

**1951:** The United States and Saudi Arabia enter into an agreement which, among other things, means that the United States will aid Saudi Arabia with military protection against Saudi Arabia selling oil priced in dollars.

**1969:** Ragnar Frisch is awarded Sveriges Riksbank's prize in memory of Alfred Nobel for his work in economics

**1971:** President Richard Nixon tells television viewers that he is going to end the US Federal Reserve's obligation to redeem dollars for gold. The US is technically bankrupt and in breach of international obligations. Economists from both the Keynesian and monetarist schools, including University of Chicago Professor Milton Friedman, predict that the price of gold will fall to 10 USD.

**1972:** The American economist James Tobin, who was also a professor at Yale University, follows up Keynes' theory and argues that inflation "greases" the economy.

**1973:** Nixon's termination of the Bretton Woods Agreement takes effect. The Americans have tripled the money supply (M2) since 1959 and the price of gold is rising to 125 USD per ounce. Nixon and Secretary of State Henry Kissinger enter into an agreement with Saudi Arabia that the US will sell weapons to Saudi Arabia in exchange for Saudi Arabia selling oil for dollars.

**1974:** Friedrich August Hayek receives the Nobel Prize in Economics.

**1976:** Milton Friedman receives the Nobel Prize in Economics.

**1981:** James Tobin receives the Nobel Prize in Economics.

**1987:** Stock markets crash all over the world, crash in the property market in Norway, emergency money for the banks.

**2008:** Financial crisis and crash in the property market in many countries, including in Norway and the US. Emergency money for the banks.

**2020-2021:** COVID-19 pandemic and even more emergency money. The global debt grows by 70%.

**2022:** The western countries are about to lose control over the rise in prices, the central banks raise interest rates and withdraw money from circulation. President Biden puts forward *The Inflation Reduction Act*, which does nothing to put an end to inflation.

Norway, one of the world's richest countries, has a government that warns that power rationing may become necessary, and is beginning to investigate measures because we may also be affected by a global food shortage. The country has gone from having a private sector that was 16 times larger than the public sector in 1900, to the public sector now spending two thirds of the GDP. 20% of all production goes into the pockets of the richest one percent of the population. Russia has invaded Ukraine. The CPI in the EU and the USA are sniffing at a 10% annual price inflation, while in Norway it currently stands at 6%. Global hyperinflation is a real possibility. In one of the economics textbooks a professor portrays it as positive that politicians can use the money illusion of inflation to trick workers into accepting wage cuts.

*The natural tendency of government,*

*once in charge of money,*

*is to inflate and destroy the value of the currency*

*

*Murray Rothbard*

Printed in Great Britain
by Amazon

32119025R00096